CHANGING MY MIND

A JOURNEY OF DISABILITY AND JOY

CHANGING *My* MIND

A JOURNEY OF DISABILITY AND JOY

CHRIS MAXWELL

Scripture quotations marked NIV are from the Holy Bible, New International Version®, copyright 1973, 1978, 1984 by International Bible Society. Used by permission of Zondervan Publishing House. All rights reserved.

Scripture taken from *THE MESSAGE* copyright© by Eugene Peterson, 1993, 1994, 1995, 1996. Used by permission of NavPress Publishing Group.

ACKNOWLEDGMENTS

Words pack these pages because many faces declared hope. The people deserve my thanks.

My Maker listened, cared, forgave, and dared. I give Him praise.

Debbie and our sons, our family members and friends and congregation, my mentors and accountability group, my amazing doctors and caregivers adjusted and assisted through my drastic changes. I thank them all.

My editors, as always, rescued me. Jamie's final work took my words and rhythm and made them better. Doree dared me to take risks with my writing. LifeSprings Resources welcomed me to dive in. And David's poetic journal turned my mourning into dancing.

To all readers with weaknesses or painful life-changes in a family member or a friend, I invite you to the dance of disease, disability and joy, to the experience of a changing of the mind. Let the music begin.

"In this book Chris Maxwell writes, 'Whatever your condition, join the journey. Enter the experience. Be aware of reality.' He has modeled how to do just that when you enter a twilight zone that distorts all you have ever known. In this case, Chris invites you to enter the twilight zone of mysterious grace. As he put it, 'join the journey.' You will not regret it!"

— Dr. A.D. Beacham, Jr.
Executive Director of Christian Education
International Pentecostal Holiness Church

"I knew Chris Maxwell before his illness, but he became my best friend after he began the slow road to recovery. The man I know today is more like Jesus—all because he faced an incredibly difficult physical challenge without ever doubting the Father's love.

This is a journal of his remarkable journey to find healing after a brain injury. You may never suffer from the effects of encephalitis, as Chris did, but we all face life-crippling weaknesses that can sideline us from God's true purpose. Whatever your personal struggle is—physical disability, emotional dysfunction, sexual brokenness or unfortunate life circumstances—Chris' insights will inspire you to press beyond the pain to reach victory."

— J. Lee Grady, Editor
Charisma Magazine

"Chris' creative, poetic nonfiction tells the testimony of his near-death experience. He takes readers into the hospital and then home to a changed life. He confesses his struggles while offering true hope found only in God. His magazine articles about the battle have encouraged many readers not to give up on God or on life. This book will touch others and help them realize their reasons for living."

— Hal Donaldson
editor of *Today's Pentecostal Evangel* and
president of Convoy of Hope

"Chris is a help to so many because he is willing to share, in real terms, his real problems, then proclaim his real victories. I am one who has received his help."

— Terry Raburn
Superintendent of the Peninsular Florida District Council
of the Assemblies of God

"What I found awesome about this book was that it very clearly described Chris' struggles, fears and victories, while giving hope to those who have struggled, are struggling, and unfortunately will struggle with similar challenges. It meshes the human struggle from a mental and medical view with the spiritual challenge of using his faith to carry him through. There is no fairy tale ending, but no crash and burn either. Just a person, with the help of family, friends and G-d, who was able to overcome an illness and return to a productive, meaningful life."

— Dr. Steven Attermann

"This is the unflinching story of a faith being severely tested and passing with flying colors. It will be deeply appreciated by people who are traveling life's hardest roads."

— Mark Atteberry, author

TABLE OF CONTENTS

Invitation: Wondering
Where the Lions Are

Most people occasionally forget a name. Spell-check and memos come in handy for us all. An appointment missed or a birthday forgotten: stuff happens. Parents stare at one child, calling him or her the name of a sibling. Singers miss words of the national anthem, or ruin Wrigley Field's seventh- inning stretch while trying to lead the fans in "Take Me Out to the Ball Game."

You've done it, haven't you? Ordered the wrong meal, taken the wrong turn, called the wrong number?

We label those errors common mistakes. Those of us who are perfectionistic control freaks condemn ourselves until we silence the self-talk. When such mistakes occur habitually, we think we're just getting old. But if blunders suddenly invade us and become the norm; if a husband knows his wife one day and doesn't the next; if a few formerly common words refuse to journey from mind to mouth; if we become a person we never hoped to be, what happens then?

I know a lot about what happens. It is still happening to me.

On these pages, I open my journal to reveal my damaged brain.

As you inspect, as you stare, as you observe, feel free to laugh at me. Cry or critique my method of survival. Think, though. Work your own mind as you glance at mine. Evaluate, calculate, assess, confess.

How do you usually respond when painful changes swirl your way? What if my journey had been yours or your spouse's? Your parent's or your pastor's? Your child's or your hero's? The President's or the homeless man's? When you are challenged by an addiction, an illness, a terrible decision—things change, don't they?

Maybe you've read about miracles but asked why your Goliath didn't go down after your best stone throw. Maybe you've prayed with faith, but every day the mirror's glass exposes a face and a life staring back, untouched by high hopes.

Maybe the sea didn't separate fully when you ran from your foes.

Now what?

Maybe you're saying, "Chris, I didn't lose my mind. I lost my child." Or "I lost my spouse," or "I lost my left leg in the war, and no one cares," or "I've got an appointment with the doctor tomorrow, and I'm very afraid," or "I've made so many stupid decisions, I think I've lost myself."

Now what?

Life, this strange mystery of joy and sorrow, includes disappointments. As my mind changed, as my life changed, as I now adjust and adapt, I'm often wondering what is out there and what is in here. On these pages, I hope we can all gather a better glance toward real life even during our journey in mystery.

My mind forgets names but remembers song lyrics and poetic stories. So each chapter in this book borrows a song's title. All of them remind me of seasons in life and of the scenes I still remember. Bruce Cockburn's tune "Wondering Where the Lions Are" took me on a tour many years ago. I started noticing the ignored, observing the forgotten, dreaming of the large. I also came to know that life really is a mystery.

Or so I thought. But now, in my unwanted exploration, I know better about life's mysteries. I know more about surviving each day. My mind helps my spiritual heart. Lyrics I hear can tell me more about lions, dreams, desires, waves, togetherness, eternity, wandering, and wondering. I can mentally digest words and determine what really has a hold on us. So can you.

In his book *The Night-Side*, Floyd Skloot defines a purpose for his words. Notice Skloot's honesty: "This book is a meditation forward and backward over the losses and gains that accompany long-term illness. Some of its pieces follow one another like chapters in a novel; others connect more associatively, like poems in a collection. It is finally an account of change and, I think, growth."[1] These pages flow in a similar current.

Change. Growth. Words we often use but rarely merge. Especially when change equals pain, sadness, grief, hurt, and an ongoing adjustment to life. We all relate. We experience changes unique to us—our own private changes. Changes noticed by others and changes ignored as long as possible by ourselves. Changes that finally, when allowed, bring growth—spiritual and relational growth, growth in thinking of others as we learn from ourselves, growth through the shrinking of ourselves.

In his book, *The Thorn in the Flesh*, R. T. Kendall writes, "Know that God has allowed this for a purpose. Accept it...as being from a loving God. Then come to terms with it. Don't pretend it's not there. Admit that it probably won't go away—at least, not for a while. God could remove it, yes, just like that! But, apart from divine intervention, come to terms with the likely fact that it is there to stay."[2]

This book collects my confessions about the growth pains and gains resulting from permanent brain damage. As you read it, write your own version. Confess your own changes, your own growth.

Whatever your condition, join the journey. Enter the experience. Be aware of reality. As you critique and confess and compare, here is the dare. Stare at me and my life to see where you are. Think of receiving help from others, of giving more when there is nothing there to give, of living. Really living.

This book is my effort to come to terms with life, with change, with a me I never expected to become. To come to terms with a me who forgets, who struggles, who doubts. I offer my own honest recovery, and I ask, What is this sad season of your life teaching you? How can your weakness make you strong?

I don't know all the answers. But my knowing so much about remembering less might help you know and do and be made new. I pray this account of thinking and changing brings growth.

Even while we're wondering where the lions are.

2 Corinthians 4:18 (NIV)
"So we fix our eyes not on what is seen, but on what is unseen. For what is seen is temporary, but what is unseen is eternal."

1

Just As I Am

"Thanks for letting me read your story."

The young woman's smile resembled applause. Her eyes brimmed with hope that I could receive her words about my writing and my illness—specifically, about my writing *about* my illness. Her tone of voice distributed deep thoughts into a packet of kind remarks and sincere confession.

"You're welcome," I said. We both paused until she talked again.

"Yeah, and thanks for writing it. That must have been hard for you."

I nodded.

Once more, I let her talk. "I've attended your church services here whenever we're in town. I knew you had to take naps and stuff like that. But I never really knew what all you have to go through. Reading what you wrote encouraged me."

Wanting to know more, I investigated how it encouraged her. Instead of asking, "How can what discourages me encourage you?" I just asked, "How?"

"My family and I struggle with Attention Deficit Disorder," she said. "The article helped me feel better about some of my own issues, I guess. So, thanks. I like your preaching and everything. But I'll like it even more now."

I thanked her as we walked in different directions.

Did she know she wasn't just a student attending a missionary school? Did she know on a summer Tuesday in

Florida she was still traveling on a mission trip she thought was completed? Did she know she served as my therapist as I battled words to write and names to recall? Did she know?

I knew.

The article told the tale of my life-changing encounter. It wasn't one of my sermons turned into readable devotionals. It wasn't one of my parables of the moon and stars illustrating biblical truth and theological arguments. The story was my story. Facts, not fiction. A near-death experience and its long-term effects: that was the story.

She doesn't subscribe to the magazine. A friend let her read it.

As she stopped me and talked, I saw so much. I said little, hearing more than she stated.

The timing made me shake my head. It had not been one of those "I can do all things through Christ" type of days. Sort of the opposite. My self-talk had just finished reminding my mind about how many names I had failed to recall during that morning's staff meeting. I used hand gestures and detailed descriptions so somebody, anybody, might catch whom I spoke of and tell me their name. Peeking in my Palm handheld is my ongoing addiction to reality. I stared at the staff as I explained to them every detail about a family. Every detail, with names not included. How could I include what I couldn't recall?

The illness that damaged my brain hit me eight years before. It hit me with no warning, sending me into a world of forgetting, suddenly transforming me from a thinker to a man learning to learn again. It appeared as my words made little sense to the listeners, as my head ached, as my thoughts failed to accomplish their duties. I feel the illness's effects daily. I know God has worked. I also know this effort to remember, to recover, to rejoice is hard work.

I must keep thanking Him as I walk in so many directions. As I think about thinking and stare back, I thank Him. It makes me better rather than bitter. I remember that phrase.

Ed, our associate pastor, talked to the staff that morning about my illness. He never knew the former me. But his medical training and brilliant mind give him the right to keep his eyes on my mind. I'm his boss, but maybe he's my rescuer. He talked about me, voicing encouragement. He argued I had progressed since he met me four years before.

"Chris is improving," Ed said. "Not depending as much on his notes or PowerPoint. He talks with an easier flow now. He worries less and just gets things done."

Gets things done? Worry less? Easier flow? Not as dependent?

Ed had mentioned similar observations when he spoke to our congregation. He articulated honest words about me, my condition, my areas of weakness. Yes, it hurt to hear the truth. And yes, it helped to hear the truth.

My point? We can gain so much through pain. We can grow and learn as we lose what we know.

Once I told a friend, "My immune system fumbled the ball. It cost me the game." Since then I have told myself, "Losing a game doesn't cost you the trophy."

Which of those statements shall I recall?

Worry less? Easier flow? A fumble and a game? A loss toward a championship?

We depend on directions. In life's journey, we have both experience and expectations. Habits develop. Rituals rule. Then—maybe slowly, maybe suddenly—things change.

We age. We get fat. We go bald. Slowly, life is no longer just as it was.

But changes sometimes shock us suddenly. With no symptoms, a doctor gives bad news. With no warning, a spouse confesses an affair. With no explanation, a kid runs away. With no logic, a gun goes off. With no advance notice, a worker resigns. Or, as I can hardly remember and can never forget, a body's immune system refuses to defeat a foe. A life, and the many lives connected to that damaged being, change forever.

We want to know more, to know all. We glance and we ask. We gaze and we grasp. We listen and we expect. We read and we write.

That, though, can often become the problem. Our wanting to *know* instead of wanting to *be*. Our mind instead of our spirit.

Our controlling instead of living. Our power instead of our person.

Since my sickness, I've learned of pain, of loss, of gain, of cost. And of choices. The advice of an editor clarifies a sentence. The honesty of a friend confronts motives. The healing of a mind changes a man. Especially if that healing begins as the sickness hits. We rarely see it that way. Can't we, though? Can't we see that painful turns and tumbles are essential for the complete tour?

An illness can cause a person to lose the use of portions of the brain. An illness can also offer an opportunity to glare at what might be a gain.

Another word rhymes and fits: pain. Blood tests are fun for me – until I hear my cholesterol count. MRIs don't bother me – that is my prayer closet. Sore muscles from a workout boost my ego. Though I find no pleasure in pain itself, outcomes earn the right to bring value to the initial discomfort.

Usually. Not always. Most often it comes back to choices, to honest decisions.

In my basketball years, I loved letting my small, point-guard body get in the way and take a charge from an opposing big man. But dental work isn't my favorite pastime. Colonoscopies have me asking, "Isn't there a better way of conducting such an investigation?" My point is this: pain, to me, doesn't in and of itself equal gain. My flesh isn't that desperate for punishment. Pain often causes escape, retreat, surrender, and defeat. It comes back to choices. Reviewing the value, counting the cost, choosing to endure. And, as we reach conclusions and make productive choices, we can decide to enjoy the journey. Not just the destination. The *journey*.

When a friend offers helpful advice, the initial pain might slowly merge into education and improvement. If we allow it.

When a foe declares hateful criticism, the immediate pain might turn into anger. If we allow it.

Choices, decisions, and purpose. I listen; how will I respond? I write; how much shall I confess? I pray; what do I believe? I read the journal of my illness; can I really endure and enjoy? Confess and warn? Notice and announce?

I noticed. Parked in a lot I used a decade before, I stared near an office where I served years prior to my illness. I watched a rabbit as she leaned her head in search of breakfast. I noticed her head jerk down, then upward quickly. She allowed her ears to stand tall, announcing control and order. She inspected the ground near a lake. Her face darted down again. She came up chewing.

That pear-shaped, silver body looked both calm and nervous, both in control and much afraid, both where she belonged and a stranger on foreign soil. I related. My shape didn't match her design, but my feelings fit how I assumed she felt.

I depend on a head that searches and searches. For names, words. For instructions given only moments before. For ideas formed. For numbers known. For events experienced and aromas smelled. My mind searches and searches. Sometimes it finds.

It seeks to locate and recall. While staring at a sunrise shining in mystery, I launch reflecting dares to my wrinkled instrument of research. I often feel parked, unable to go forward. I feel like one watching, rather than one living or being. I stare, I glance, I bow, I swallow. Calm and nervous, I live. In control and afraid, I smile. At home and a stranger, I write about lessons learned.

Unlike my new rabbit friend, I rarely search for breakfast. The organized, morning man that I am – others might call me obsessive, controlling, stuck – knows what time to wake, knows where to find cereal, knows which medicine to take. Unless, of course, anything has been moved. When that happens, I search. No longer in control, I am a timid stranger, needing to learn from a rabbit.

Unable to locate what I want and need, I am no longer comfortable. I'm slowly learning, though, that my Maker wants me there. There. In person and aware of reality. A rabbit facing risks, knowing I no longer know as much as I did. There, living in an inner village I never hoped to locate, living as a person without all the answers or all the cures or all the victories. But still, living there. As I continue recovering and adjusting, I must depend on what He can do for me. My story is not just about me. It is about Someone Else who saved me. Someone Else who is still saving me from myself. During this non-stop surgical procedure of ongoing changes, I often want to jerk my head like a rabbit avoiding danger. I prefer to hop quickly toward a hideout or be very silent, still and concealed by my surroundings so that no one can notice my real self. Or just continue eating, pretending nothing else matters but the moment and the feeling.

I've always known better. I've always been taught never to live that way. But now, I know so much more.

Walking near my rabbit friend, I wanted to tell her what I wrote. Stopping to avoid her fearful escape, I confessed more of myself to the Rabbit Maker. Looking toward the office of my past, I worked to recall. I praised the Listener for caring and for daring.

***

The young lady said to me, "Thanks for letting me read your story."

Ed said to an audience, "Chris is doing better in a lot of ways."

I imagined the rabbit saying to herself, "Chris is watching. He thinks he might forget me. But I think he will remember."

Am I willing to say to God, "Thanks for letting me live this story?"

If not, I might be losing more than memory

2

Someone Saved My Life Tonight

L iving the story isn't simple. Gaining through losing isn't fun. But looking back in time is important for growth and recovery. Improvement needs truth. I can look back at my moments of change. I can try to relearn. I can try to rejoice. I can try to remember.

How did it begin?

Living in the now, I remember the story.

***

I expected a typical Tuesday.

At the office early, I talked, read, wrote, and studied. Goals and agenda knew their places. The week waited, my plans set on the stage of assumptions, of routine. I planned to see faces, to say words, to solve problems.

My body chose to change those plans.

After feeling tired and weak all afternoon, I grew worse. That night I assumed I had the flu.

The next day I stayed home on a Wednesday much different from all my previous midweek moments. I cancelled my breakfast with Tim. My comments confused listeners. When I called the office and complained to our administrator about the condition of our steeple, people worried. And wondered, "What steeple?" When I informed my sons that their pet rabbits ran inside, they worried. And wondered, "What rabbits?"

Healthy Chris didn't have a steeple or rabbits. He didn't have a doctor either. Relatives suggested a physician. The short visit yielded no conclusion. I became worse.

My wife Debbie remembers more: "You couldn't get up and just decided to stay in bed. You said you had the worst headache of your life. Felt queasy. Couldn't eat. I kept checking on you, but you would never get up. You said that Shaq needed to play for Georgia Tech. You complained about the church's steeple on the phone. When I heard a loud noise, I thought one of the boys had hit something while playing basketball outside. A few minutes later, I went to check on you and found you getting off the floor. You had passed out. I left to call my mother."

Afternoon appointments to help counsel my friends? Cancelled. Attending our Wednesday night church gathering to hear my missionary friend Larry Myers? Deb and the boys went. I convinced her to go while I stayed home. And became worse.

My formerly healthy body lost consciousness and fell again to the floor. One crash broke a basket packed with magazines. Would I read them again? Would I write in them again? I didn't know what else inside me was falling, crashing, breaking.

Thursday came. I couldn't speak at the local school and present the story of hope. I couldn't lead a church staff meeting and guide the team as their leader. I couldn't keep any counseling appointments. I couldn't do any of my normal life routines. Why? My life was no longer normal. My words made no sense. My emotions threatened to erupt. My life felt interrupted, intruded, robbed. Those feelings were just the beginning.

Inside? I felt strange emotions. Fear. Confusion. Desperation. Dizziness. And still I felt so weak, so tired, so different from any previous episode in my 35 years.

Debbie knew it was time, maybe past time, to take me to the hospital. She didn't expect me to agree. I did. We dropped our three sons off at her parents' house. Were they worried, afraid, confused? In denial? I connected to each piece of that mix: worry, fear, confusion. Merging those elements with denial, I rode toward a land of radical change: tall mountains, fierce storms, hard rocks, sharp cliffs, and dark clouds. Or, to forget the imagery, let's word it like this: I rode to the emergency room to see if my life would be saved.

I saw so little then and there. I knew nothing of what I would soon know. This mixed-up man motioned for Deb to turn east. The hospital where I normally served as a caregiver waited for us. A shifting of my role. The pastor would become a patient? The healer and helper needed healing, help? The rescuer desperate to be rescued?

As Deb drove, I shook, stared. Feeling pain, I didn't know the journey my body was traveling. My open eyes roved. Staring at the road, glancing at traffic, I knew where we were riding, but I didn't know where our lives were going. My dizzy head digested the events of a moment. They placed me in the hospital, the place to become my new home.

Doctors and nurses listened to words flowing from a preacher's mouth. Oh, I could still talk. And talk I did. They hoped to translate my phrases into explanations. They desired to rescue this angry, confused young man. Not much was working.

Had I overdosed on drugs? My actions and emotions gave such an appearance. A nurse from our congregation argued with her staff, saying, "Chris isn't like that." They had heard of other preachers, public personas, who became what audiences thought they could never become. But this lady knew better, and they trusted her.

Then tests. Machines made to investigate, critique, categorize, suggest cures. Machines designed for minds like mine. A high temperature, a confused brain, a virus on the move. They located the curse. They searched for a cure.

Deb can't forget that night. She remembers: "I watched you deteriorate. You tried to talk, but it sounded like scrambled eggs. I kept thinking, 'Why is he doing this?'"

Think about it. We can call it a near-death experience without the imagery, the music, the magic. Whatever we call it, I chose a strange role. Instead of welcoming the rescuers, I debated them. Instead of accepting the tests, I argued against my need. The doctors reached a conclusion. I could sign a paper

not holding them responsible for my death. I gave in. They
dived in. Their work started working.

It worked too slowly for me, though. Expecting a quick fix
and a move back home, I spoke often. My phrases faded from
fact to fiction, from clear to confusing, but I didn't notice.

Nurses nodded. I thought they understood me.

Nurses worked. I thought they turned against me.

I thought I could still think. The brain cells had other plans:
mingling phrases normally distant from each other, pausing
when I needed them to hurry, hiding words while not notifying
me of their disappearance.

Deb remembers the doctors recommending more tests: "I
called my mother again and said, 'They are keeping him at the
hospital. Something is really wrong. They just don't know what
it is.' Then I called your father and told him everything, but
also asked him not to come to Orlando until we knew more."

I recall little of that night. My notes come from tales told
to me, stories voiced about me. Yet this mind found a way
to record and recall my first of many MRIs. Looking back, I
remember the room of the unknown.

My dreaming-while-awake continued as the machine
inspected the electrical system sheltered by my skull. That
brain-under-review reached its own conclusions. *The group of
ladies kidnapped me,* I thought. They wanted to run tests on me
that I didn't need. A body of sweat swept from bed to bed,
gadget to gadget, glance to glance. A nightmare letting me only
stare. I had no control. I feared who did. That wouldn't be my
final expedition with magnetic resonance imaging.

My memory only grasps a portion, a short segment of the
scene. Surrounded by strangers, I remember feeling trapped,
betrayed, attacked. Why did I view those working to determine
my problem as opponents?

Isn't that life for so many of us so much of the time? Those
moments when we cannot cure our issues and have to trust
others to guide us, test us, and bring relief? Remembering only
moments of that live dream, can I learn from the scene? Can I
turn toward knowing that many more drivers will help me get

where I need to go, and many more tests will determine my realness? Or will I today seek to fight back as I did that night?

Faces and voices and too many people around me. I remember. But that is all I recall.

They returned me to my new dwelling place. A room, a location, a rescue mission. My new home for my new life. I could call it a born-again experience, but that would sound too nice. I could label it a life-changing experience, but that would limit the price.

What was Debbie doing and thinking? "My thoughts at first were denial. I really never thought you were going to die, until the doctor said it. That was unthinkable.

"We'll just get a shot of something then go home,' I thought. When they decided to keep you and did the spinal tap, I thought, 'Something must really be wrong.' Around 10:00 I met with Dr. Pineless. He told me they thought it was a stroke, seizures, both, or encephalitis. He said they would do more tests to find out, but he asked me many questions about your lifestyle, your stress level, and things like that. Then Dr. Pineless asked me all those questions, and I was wracking my brain to see if there was some weird thing you had been doing lately that I didn't know about that was causing this. Were you counseling too many people and it drove you crazy? I was confident that you weren't doing drugs. Stroke? Weren't you too young? I even called Steve Brennan at 11:30 at night to see if you had been hit in the head by a basketball in the game the night before. I saw you when you returned from the MRI.

"I was puzzled by the whole process. Kind of numb. I felt like I was sitting back watching someone else's life on TV, and it would all be okay in about an hour when the show was done. Things like this just didn't happen to me or my family. Never had. Then as they kept you in the hospital day after day, my thoughts shifted to how I was going to make it, keep it all together, and how were you going to be different. I didn't want to question God; I just really tried to trust Him. I went to pray with the boys at my parents' house. I let them stay there, and I went home to sleep by myself."

After reviewing the tests, the doctors decided what to call it. A name I had never known before. A name I struggled to remember then. A name I will never forget: encephalitis.

The calendar called it March 1996. My body chose a different march, a lonely march, a march rushing me into unfamiliar territory. The journey of encephalitis crushed me.

The typical Tuesday and week and year I expected? They never came. Every waiting Tuesday held a flavor of that week's war. Every week and year since then have kept me near that pain, that place, that encephalitis.

My life knew only health before that. My childhood memories—scenes circling then in my mind as brain cells searched for nonfiction, for historic, personal facts during my recovery—knew about sicknesses of others, but only health for me. But then, a man who couldn't remember the names of his three sons searched for recovery. I tried to think about things. I tried to think. I had never tried that hard before.

Would I remember my sons' names? Would they remember the old me? Would they like the new me? I asked as I stared. I cried as doctors and nurses tested and worked on the new me.

Deb remembers more: "Everyone wanted to check on you, but we couldn't let them visit. I called your father again and told him he needed to come. Chris, you were really sick. Your dad made it in five hours. Your sisters also came from Georgia. You remembered faces but not names. My brother Stan came in and left very upset. He said, 'This isn't right. It's not supposed to happen to him.'"

My jerking face, my shaking lips, my wet eyes, my uncontrolled remarks: Where was God during that time? Maybe He told me where, and I just couldn't recall. Maybe I already knew but just couldn't remember. Since my ears received sound waves but got little help from the brain's reception, maybe God's answer remained undiscovered in mysterious terrain.

I could only pray and hope God heard. Pray and hope. Pray. And hope.

I thought of my thinking as I worked to realize and remember.

3

Lights

The lights had gone down in my inner city.

I kept praying, hoping God kept hearing. I kept working to realize and remember, to think of my thinking.

Hospitals reside in irregular time zones. They send minds back or forward. My mind wasn't sure what to do, nor was I sure what it was doing. At that moment, though, I ventured way back in history. To Mama, to meals, to seasons, to stories.

In that new home, in that home I didn't purchase or pick, I recalled an old, old residence. A home or a house? A world wide or a few steps long? Its size felt big to me as a little blond boy in northeast Georgia.

I remember learning about the brain in elementary school. Human brains impressed me. Picking that topic for a science fair, I learned so much about learning. Back then I bought a brain model whose pictures and images didn't match modern technology's precision. Still, visual explanations impressed me as I let the study teach my brain about itself.

My mother liked my brain display. Her Southern vocabulary sneaked out as she smiled and listened to my rehearsal of the speech. If I had known in the science fair what I know now, I might have asked, "Can I buy a brain?" I could have kept it in storage.

Back then, my brain and I cooperated to learn. I liked that style of learning better than how I did it in the new land of

my battlefield. This time I battled in my brain. That method
of sending images as messages didn't catch time's expected
rhythm, I concluded slowly as mental images raced through.
The experience educated and depressed the confused me. What
could that research now teach me about myself?

And Mama? She wasn't with me this time, though. This
wasn't a study, a quiz, an assignment, a science fair. There
didn't seem to be much about it that felt fair. If Mama had
been in the hospital with me, would she have smiled? Would
she have helped me smile again? Would she have explained
in her country chatter that it was only a study, a quiz, or an
assignment? Would she have helped me pass?

What was going on? Where was she when I needed her? She
wasn't there. She now lived in a land with no viruses and no
MRIs. She wasn't there to observe or to hold. She had left long
before. And I felt so alone.

My Mama wasn't there.

But a nurse walked in, smiling. She asked questions I tried
to answer. Again, I couldn't. I promised her, "I normally know
things; I'm not really stupid." She smiled, trying to calm me.
She wanted to convince me she knew. Did she?

Though busy, she took time to notice my intense grief. Not
only physical and mental pain, but also emotional pain. I felt
disappointed. I had enjoyed living with answers, decisions,
honesty, information, effort, action. At that moment, I could
breathe, look, live. Listen but not understand. Talk but not
make sense.

She left me. I knew she planned to return. So much else had
left me. I didn't know how much planned to return.

My wife and sons and friends wondered. At that moment I
existed. No more? No less? Not knowing more or less or any
portion of the rest, I breathed. I breathed. I talked without
making sense. I saw without grasping the view. I felt, felt, felt. I
cried and asked to leave as I stared, wondered, and wanted.

Moments of time equaled mysteries.

Once I shared my mysteries from Room 110. In the middle of
the night, I decided I had been there long enough. I untied my

arms from my medical attachments; I set myself free. Free at last and dressed for the occasion.

I walked out of my room only wearing my shirt—a preacher with no pants. A patient with no mind. I spoke to a nurse at the desk who calmly panicked and quickly called my nurse for the night. Thinking my words made sense to her, I stood staring as she listened.

Later she gave me a new title, one I wish I could forget. In Bible college, they never taught us to influence the world by serving as "the preacher with the cute butt." My new name let the nurses smile. My family needed humor and gladly received what my midnight march provided.

That event, frightening then but funny now, proved how "crazy" I had become. I remembered that word, asking if they thought I had become that. They didn't answer with words. But their attempts to cover their expressions didn't work. I had become crazy to them.

My brain wasn't functioning correctly. And I didn't know it.

Looking back on my stroll toward the nurses' station, people can laugh at my mistakes and remarks. People can laugh. But then and there, fear flavored most of our emotions. And it wasn't funny for me at that moment. Especially when they locked me in for the night. They decided to take no more chances with my walking ventures. Tied to the bed, I stayed. Julia saw and heard my weaknesses. Having a nurse who believed in God helped me adjust to the me I worked to notice. Helping the perspective of her impatient patient, Julia made a huge difference; I couldn't voice my appreciation. She says, "When I left your room and glanced back, you had already looked away."

Adjustments dashed in my direction. A world I ignored left and began to return. Now it is funny to see how I learned to eat, to talk, and to live all over again.

I reached for the ice cream with a fork. I stuttered my excitement to Deb, asking, "You ever tasted this before? This is good!"

"Yes," she calmly replied, "It's ice cream. You like it."

Beginning to eat the spaghetti with my finger, I complained, "This is messy."

Deb handed me a fork and suggested, "Try using this."

Deb also had new hopes about her new man. Maybe my forgetfulness just might help her turn me into a much better guy. Maybe, for instance, she could convince me that I loved onions. No luck. The nurse brought meatloaf for dinner one night, and I slowly researched the meal. Very cautiously, I located the onions and destroyed them. I placed a pile of those unneeded vegetables beside my plate, realizing the fork had value after all and could separate the wanted from the unwanted.

Debbie watched my serious self and glanced at her new life. Life?

When Deb's brother and sister-in-law came in to see me, I talked. Actually, I preached, reminding them of the importance of loving each other, of living for God, of not messing up. Joe, at that time a professional baseball player, had left spring training to check on us. He and his wife nodded as I talked, so they tell me. I trust what they say. I remember none of it.

When my father came, I could not call him Pops. I smiled, though. He turned and walked away, crying. He smiled when I told him I liked his shirt. He later bought me one just like it. I still don't remember.

The clock in the hospital room, I argued, was always wrong. Deb and the nurses thought the clock was a machine checking my blood pressure, but what did they know? They should have trusted me; my name was at the door.

***

Life, like meals, can be messy. Especially when we only trust the name at the door. Especially when we think we are okay. Especially when we think we know so much.

Deb says, "When the boys saw you, they were scared. They didn't know what to expect. You cried frequently."

Everything amazed me, the things I always took for granted before my illness. Debbie explained to me the purpose of toilets and toilet tissue. It amazed me. A person can sit naked in a chair's open seat, let the body do what it needs to do, clean up and push a button for an event called flushing?

And meals. I hold tools with strange names like *fork* and *spoon* and *knife*, snatch soft or hard items of yellow or green or dark brown that might taste delicious or might make me sick again, and then carry those things to my mouth to determine their worth, for the plan of swallowing and digesting them?

And showers. I can stand naked—this time by approval—in a clear cave and turn on water to enjoy the drizzle?

When Debbie vowed for better and for worse, did she think I would one day be that clumsy, that crude, that childish? When she observed the new me, did she assume I would get better quickly and revert to the former man? Did she know I would never again remember names as before, or that a few dishes would always get placed in the wrong cabinets after being washed, or that I would go to bed early for the rest of our marriage?

Those days, in that place, she let her face display grace. The crying was my uncontrolled technique. Her tears hid; she saved them for only a chosen few to view.

***

I can remember a night alone, when a nurse turned out the lights in my room. Awake in darkness, questions crammed my anxious mind.

That night owned me. Sleep wanted nothing to do with my illness or my life. My inside feelings, I thought, found possibilities. I could stay and do nothing. Or I could walk and think, working to figure out my new life. Like life: stay and do nothing, or walk and work to figure things out. Staying in the room kept me quiet. Staying in the room pushed more answerless questions in a mental circle of uncertainty. The machines had been disconnected; they no longer held me back, so I climbed out of bed and walked toward a window in the hall.

I sat on a chair by that window, that opening from my cave to a free world, the view reminding me of a life I could barely remember. I enjoyed my new place.

Parked cars. Traffic, toward Orlando or from, still rolling
that late on that night. For a moment, they came into my sight,
and then they journeyed past me with no effort to notice a
patient staring from a window. I couldn't call them or control
them. They were busy. I was blocked. I sat and watched. Sat
and watched.

I had expected to go home that day, but my body
temperature didn't drop enough. It stayed at 103.3. They waited.
Could only the 98.6 code unlock me, release me, send me home?

I questioned a lot of things while living in that hospital
room. Looking back now, I compare my complaints to those
of victims locked in war or poverty or hospitals for long times.
My scuffle with sickness could have been so much worse. Then,
though, I thought 10 days equaled a very long time.

I wrote. *Sleep. Or not sleep. Leave a bed in the night's middle
moment to look outside. I can pretend to be driving and laughing. I can
pretend to know people and their names.* I tried to work through my
feelings of being owned by my questions. I cried as I wondered.
Looking outside as I thought of my inside self, my old self, my
new self. As I thought of life and death, of past and future, I
could pretend. And ask. And think. And blink, facing reality
and me. This me. This me I worked to meet and know and love.
Awake. Or not awake. A moment of looking into the middle of
my mind and asking myself questions. A moment of listening
for the Maker of my life and asking Him honest questions.
Looking outside, looking inside, I thought.

Feelings and fears twisted me, turned me. But did they *own*
me? No. I laughed as I returned to my room. "No day owns
me," I announced to myself, fervent to believe it. "No night
owns me."

Pain pushed, but I could push back. The way to do that, I
realized, was to pray. The nurse smiled as I crawled into my
bed, hoping for sleep.

Instead I prayed. Praying left me hoping, even while I
dreamed.

4

One More Night

That night, hoping, I prayed about what had left me. I prayed about dreams. I dreamed about prayers. It would not be the last night.

I'm not alone in the world of reliving and reworking. So many of us look back and find pain. So many of us glance into the history book hidden by our denial or despair or damaged brain, and we smile or we weep. We feel alive or dead. We want to stay awake or quickly fall asleep again.

Post-traumatic stress disorders present flashbacks. The reality of those moments make victims feel like past disasters are occurring again. It is not just recalling traumas. Bodies panic, feeling trapped as intense sensations notice a perpetrator. Dreaming outside the range of normal human experience, such flashbacks put us in a place where we need to find allies, not opponents.

I'm not an expert. But I do pose an argument for our memories and our moments. Surprising, painful dreams will come. Unexpected nightmares will wake us. Memories and voices will shake us. There is also a positive view of flashbacks, dreams, thoughts. Can't we choose to design new thoughts and great thoughts and joyful thoughts? Can't we awake in the middle of our sleepy life and choose to recall reality? Can't we remind ourselves of true meaning and purpose, of elements of reality, of sins forgiven, of burdens needing to be released?

The electrical system of our brains is often tricky. So is that system of the physical hearts and the spiritual hearts. So is that system of relationships, desires, choices, and results. We sleep, and we awaken. We lie down, and we jump up. We notice a fan rotating and a mate breathing. We ask for answers and hear silence. We want to be left alone and feel covered by noise. That is life. For all of us. All of us, each disabled in our general way as fallen man, each disabled in specific ways which only belong to us.

But we can think it through. Rather than retreating and being defeated, we can choose to wake from our selfness, our state of being, our disability, our stress. We can wake and smile. We can walk, pray, sing, and laugh. Eyes can see each day as new. Ears can hear noises and pause for a smile. Inner beings can dare the mind to mind us, refusing to let disabilities destroy our true abilities to adjust, adapt, and rejoice amid our mental power outages.

That one night I woke and remembered. I returned to sleep, hoping to remember. I didn't. But I think I can still remember a lesson. Wishing I would wake again tonight or tomorrow night and remember all I have forgotten, I can still remember a lesson learned. No matter what happens tonight, I can still remember.

***

Nights and days passed in that hospital. Meals came. Nurses worked. Doctors talked and asked. The dreamer didn't know much; he only pretended to know the answers to their questions.

No, I couldn't remember the President's name. Yes, I liked the doctor's tie and correctly guessed one of three colors. Yes, I could remember my Social Security number. No, I couldn't recall the names of my sons. No, I couldn't figure out why so many relatives and friends wanted to visit Orlando, stare at me, cry, pray. Yes, I knew Georgia Tech was playing a basketball game on TV that night. No, I couldn't read the stats on the screen.

Dialogues equaled disasters. Questions invited my rambling, my rolling, my rampaging. I tried to be smart, to be funny, but my communication lacked common sense. The sense that had been common to me became absent. Facts hid in faraway places. Crowded with workers and friends, crying to God, I felt alone. I wanted to go home.

***

These days, I realize how so many people still live that way. Not always in hospitals unsure of their words. Not always the center of caring attention. But their frowns confirm inner frustrations. Unvoiced questions pack the mental baggage and leave hurting people crammed with concealed pain. Picture people like me and people like you hiding from reality and refusing to acknowledge truth. Concerns can crowd us. We all need healing, approval, and care.

***

During my time in the hospital, Debbie held her concerns deep inside. She packed them and kept them covered. A few tears sneaked out, but only at appropriate times and in appropriate places. Her mother, remembering one of those moments, says, "She came to the house broken, crying, asking questions. She didn't know how to handle what was happening. She fell on the floor at the foot of my bed and said, 'He can't die. He can't die. He is just so sick. He doesn't know me; he doesn't know anybody. He thinks everybody is out to get him.'"

Her face in the hospital reflected the expressions of a mother taking care of a baby. A counselor giving a client hope. A sergeant preparing a soldier for battle. Debbie, the spouse of a wounded man, tried; I cried.

As days came, as days left, I continued scribbling my thoughts. Were they thoughts or feelings? What were they? I didn't know. I knew I needed to release them. Three days of poorly spelled honesty helped me release frustration, assisted me to remember faith in a Father.

I used pencil and paper to keep a journal: *Feeling, not believing. Waiting and wishing. Asking, not knowing. Wanting and wondering.* I wrote without wisdom. No king of Israel, of course; still, I followed David's Psalmistic course: honesty to the God who already knows how we feel. Why fake it?

Some Christians teach us that faith equals lying. Biblical faith faced difficulty, knew frustration, hated struggles, and still trusted a powerful Master. Me? I knew little. Me? I needed help. Me? I tried to call on my Helper, my Healer. He understood my writing, reading misspelled words that my previous pride would never have put on display. He cared. He came. Later, He cured. But then and there, I needed to proclaim what I could hardly describe.

Months later, I worked to read and learn more about myself, a me I hardly knew. I wanted to know why I struggle with my memory. I slowly read about "a rare but serious infection," about "inflammation of the brain cells." Complex descriptions defined my problem and challenged me to comprehend.

Signs and symptoms? Drowsiness, disorientation, confusion, seizures, sudden fever, severe headache, nausea and vomiting, tremor, stiff neck. Emergency symptoms? Altered levels of consciousness.

I knew, I knew. I could remember. Personal experience.

Tell me more. Tell me more.

Encephalitis? A rare, acute inflammatory disease of the brain caused by viral infection. Close to two thousand cases per year in America. In 1996, I was one of the chosen.

I read on until I found comments about my type of encephalitis. Can be particularly deceptive when it starts as a minor illness bringing headaches or fevers. Difficulty talking, weakness, confusion, unconsciousness, seizures.

Was my condition serious? Often. Acute days may last a week or two weeks. Changes may come slowly. Maybe a short duration and benign. Maybe severe with significant mental impairment, including loss of memory, inability to speak coherently, lack of muscle coordination, paralysis, hearing or vision defects.

So I have some. I could be so much worse.

Death? Mortality varies. Some survive, some do not. I did.

Future? Rest, nourishment. Physical and speech therapies could help those left with mental impairment. Reading about me then confused me even more.

But I kept reading. My type of this illness? "Dangerous," I read. "Sometimes fatal," I read. "Encephalitis is often fatal, begins abruptly, can cause seizures, mental changes, and rapid onset of coma."

I read more. I thought more. I thanked God more. Slowly.

The reading and studying and listening offered me time to investigate myself. Research revealed facts of my struggles. It slowly defined for me the new word in my life, the word describing my new life: *encephalitis*. Pages informed me of its meaning, of how it served as a virus from an unsure cause and worked as the catalyst for changing my mind, of how it hits people in my country two thousand times each year, of how many face permanent damage. Slowly, I continued to read about me. Noticing words of definition and description, I compared those pages to myself and my new life. I read about patients losing consciousness; I remembered what they told me about my early days. I read about disorientation, dizziness, and death; I remembered what they told me, what I could recall, and I realized again a miracle had happened to me. Though reading about a lifetime of tests, mental impairment, struggles to remember, paralysis, vision and hearing defects, I could understand and think and pray. Though reading slowly about an abrupt and often fatal illness, about its results of seizures and comas and divorce and depression and addiction and death, I was still breathing. Slowly, I was reading about how I had become part of a new tribe. Another word beginning with E told me about me. *Epilepsy*. That was the result of my *encephalitis*.

That, though, was months later. Then and there, I understood so little. Praying often, thinking about thinking, battling the facts with the feelings, seeking to grasp myself, I ventured into the frequently forbidden land of asking God why. *Why can't I know that friend's name? Why can't I spell the words that come to my mind? And, my mind, my mind, will it ever be the same? The shame I feel leads me to wonder if we had made a deal and I failed my portion of the agreement. They've told me before. So many of them have told me before. I've told myself before: Don't ask God why. But why? Why can't I ask You why? You are the One Who Knows. You are the One Who Cares. Even if You don't answer, maybe it will help me to ask. Wouldn't it? Couldn't it? Father, may I? Was it my lack of faith that caused a disease? Has sin put me in a spell of waiting for me to become a better person before being healed? Or am I just one of many people who hurt, who cry, who fail to recall? And am I just one of many who needs You, who needs You today? Not Your answers or Your explanations or Your solutions or Your miracles. You. Just You. Maybe that is the Ultimate Answer to my unlimited questions. Maybe You are.*

That, though, was later. In the hospital I never knew if I would read again. During my worst times, I wondered why God let it happen, why God let it happen to *me*. During better times that would come much later, I wondered why God sent just enough of a healing to keep me alive. I wrote in my journal: *Wondering about this wonder. God is wonderful. Full of wonder?*

See how my thoughts twisted and turned? See how the dot-by-dot pace of rhythm curved dialogue and description?

My inmost thoughts, though hiding from view or trouncing around uncontrollably, wanted to decide. Asking myself questions didn't provide answers. But I kept asking, wanting to know: Is this working? Is this really working?

Some portions of my honest journal echo memoirist Annie Dillard's rhythmic words. In *An American Childhood,* Dillard writes of the back and forth, give and take awakening that all children undergo: "I woke in bits, like all children, piecemeal over the years. I discovered myself and the world, and forgot them, and discovered them again."[3] Her words explain my seasonal shifts. For me, they had nothing to do with aging. Then and there, so suddenly, I sought to discover. To find me. To find life. To find.

In bits, I worked to live.

Many friends came to visit, to find out, to find me. They watched and observed. In bits, they found some of me.

During my sickness, I needed help to keep me from focusing too far below God, only on my pain. Honesty is certainly okay with God. He handles it fine since He already knows how we feel. No honesty surprises Him. The openness allows us to enter His presence without pretending. By subtracting our acting, we can enjoy a closeness to God that we need and He desires. That unity with Him was what I needed then. My past had taught me of it and I had longed for it, prayed for it, believed it by faith, and enjoyed it many times. Then, in a war for life, I needed Him and needed to remember He wanted to be close to me.

Why does that surprise us?

As I prayed in the hospital room, I looked high to the center of the ceiling. I stared and talked to God. I asked Him why. I never heard an answer with my ears. My heart sensed reminders I needed: "*I am with you.*" God regularly asserted His presence in that place where I found myself and my pain. He was there with me.

I believed Him. I heard no voice, but I knew He remained with me. He *was* so good, and He *is* so good. I pray that in my more pleasant, comfortable existence, I will reach toward Him with the eagerness that drove me in that hospital room. Will I?

***

One night, board members from Evangel Assembly, the church I still pastor, came to the hospital to pray for me. Their pastor, who believes in miracles and prayer and healing, was not a healthy man. That was before the doctors knew everything that was going on, but they knew my condition was serious. Those friends cared. Their love lifted them toward our Father; they prayed with hope, faith, concern. A nurse soon told them to leave. I hardly knew them; I only called one by name. I looked, listened. Their faces broadcast what my face told them: I wasn't myself.

Those men cared, and they would continue to encourage our loving church to care. So many called, hoping to visit me, but they could not. Lifting prayers helped them, helped me, and allowed God to hear the confessions released.

Our Father longs for us to lean on Him when weakness covers our conditions. Nights like that night seem like dreams. Bad dreams. Living nightmares. God knew everything, though, so calling on Him was the right thing. The sure thing. My friends from church, from so many places, called on Him. That night I was glad for God, though I may not have revealed it.

***

My sisters, Janet and Laura, came from Georgia to visit. Janet and her husband, Bruce, had stayed with us the weekend before my strangeness began. Now, during this odd shift of my life, Laura and her husband, Martin, came, bringing Janet, visiting me for different reasons. No vacation now. They came to help; they came with hope.

Through my whole life, God blessed me with a great family. My sisters, though too much older than me for us to spend lots of time together during our younger years, treated me well, and I them. We lived through normal family issues, but our family seemed different. My sisters, my dad, and I believed my mother. She lived in such sincere love it shone humor to us, life to us, God to us. She taught us to say no to negatives, but, unlike so many who do that, her strength came in teaching us to say yes to positive points of life.

In that room that had been my prison, my sisters, of course, talked about Mama. They knew I remembered her name, never forgot it. We laughed about what she would say; we cried about my pain that needed her—not in heaven, but with me at that moment. We trusted God while feeling our emotions shift quickly, sharply. In me, through me. I had changed, but they stayed with me. How hard was it for them? I wondered.

Janet, the oldest child, lives as an oldest child. She pursues perfection, expects cooperation, and struggles with those who cannot grasp proper living. That, of course, promises good and bad moments, but Janet uses her banners as blessings. She leads herself for the good of all, not simply for the glory of self.

With me there in that time, she seemed only caring, loving, worried about me.

Laura, the middle child, lives as a middle child. She performs popularly, delivers humor, and cannot understand why some people take life too seriously. That, too, offers positive and negative outcomes, but Laura uses her laughter as love. She longs to lift others, and not just to bless herself with fun moments.

With me, there in this time, she seemed only caring, loving, worried about me.

Together, they made a difference for me. We enjoyed each other, laughing to replace the tears, praising God when we knew we should and could. Janet and I laughed at a problem Laura went through. We will never forget it and never stop laughing about it. Laura did not laugh immediately, but later she did, and always will.

Personal family, church family; most people felt like family. They visited. They prayed. More people came and cared. One friend remembers seeing me stare and say nothing. One friend remembers hearing me say, "Please keep praying. I don't know what's really going on here." They continued praying. I continued working to know, and that process is evident in my journal. *So many others live beside me in this new home, this hospital, this center of recovery, the surgical discovery of life and change and lives so much the same. They live in rooms on this same floor on this same hall, but who sees them there? Who prays for them? I wasn't sure about myself; I felt like a stranger in a world of mystery. But I wasn't alone. Others, those still normal and still themselves, came to see me and to care. But those strangers living in rooms near me in this world? Who has come to care? Who is there to stare? How can I share my lovers with the world so nearby?*

5

It's a Family Affair

Ten days was more than long enough for me. And, finally, my body and my doctors and my future caught up with my thinking. I could go home. My temperature hit the magic number, but would I be able to remember how to live away from the comforts and constant care? Or was there a Comforter who had promised to always be there, constantly caring for me? I thought so. Now, I know so.

The doctors and nurses said goodbye. They gave gifts; they prayed prayers; they reminded me of my walk down the hall while undressed for the occasion. My father, still in Orlando, planned to drive me home. To see my sons, to see my house, to see what life was like before my rebirth. I would be back where I wanted to be. Debbie's parents visited, watched our sons, talked, listened, served food, prayed, and wondered what would happen next.

After one more night at Florida Hospital East, my father took me home to my wife and sons. Our Heavenly Father was with us in the car and waiting for us at home.

He had been there all along.

On that Saturday, a day that waited so long to come visit me, I sat on my bed in the hospital room. Waiting. My Dad was there. Basil and Kathy, one of my close pastor friends and his wife, were there. We joked and smiled as they knew I wanted to leave. Home seemed better than ever.

Those times were hard, but permission to leave thrilled me.

A nurse walked by. She smiled. "Only a few more minutes."

The nurses and doctors who walked with me through this illness blessed me. Doctors Lee Adler, Steven Attermann, Hal Pineless, the nurses, and so many others offering themselves to me, helped so much. They didn't just perform jobs; they worked for me, on me. Putting up with my peculiar mind, they gave listening ears, offered strong direction, and dealt with my condition. They *cared*.

I spoke to them about my job and my God. Some knew Him, some did not; but they didn't turn away and avoid my voice. They didn't debate; they listened to a sick man preaching as he went home from the hospital. Some even cried, asking me to pray for them. Were they just being politically correct? Were they afraid the sick man might attack? Or were they hoping that the Rescuer who saved my life could also help them?

One nurse, Alexia, had given me a gift when I moved from the first floor to the fifth floor. She had helped me and endured remarks from my lost brain. This time, watching me leave the hospital, she gave me another gift, a green frog doll. The new me took it home, wondering what else I was bringing.

As I left the hospital, I felt like a little kid. Glad with a strange gladness, a type of joy matching none of my past moments. I had always considered myself a joyful person, but this time joy came in a different way. Along with that joy I felt weak but pleased. The trip home led me to pray, thank God, look forward, wonder, watch, ask questions of my Dad, wonder why it all happened, glance at the scar on my arm and wonder about others, stare, rejoice.

Walking in the door of our house thrilled me; entering my own place encouraged me. But seeing my boys excited me. My sons' expressions indicated that they felt unsure. Their looks toward their mother before answering my questions. Their glances toward their new father before they realized their body language had an ability to voice its feelings. Pauses, forced smiles, assigned hugs, delays. They didn't know how to act, but that was okay. I related; I felt totally unsure too. I talked to them, took walks with them. I slept often, not realizing my body planned to sleep every afternoon for the rest of my life.

Annie Dillard writes, "We wake, if we ever wake at all, to mysteries, rumors of death, beauty, violence."[4] Annie is right: "Mysteries, rumors of death, beauty, violence." The commotion isn't always kept apart; I felt life's extremes hitting at once.

Life comes. It is. Then it leaves. While here, it changes. Varieties of circumstances and choices guide and decide the changes. Unexpected and unwanted alterations arrive. No choice channels it. No real reason directs it. But change comes.

I still breathe, I would think. *I still have this body. I am still here. But a changed me, a new me, a* different *me is still here. And often, to grasp it all, I am still. Just still.*

Only a few more minutes? Or a few months? Years? Or a never-changing change? I asked those types of questions. My family's noisy silence, their facial expressions, their eye contact with each other, the comments they thought I couldn't hear, and their caution all spoke about the world they had entered. They worked to make things work. They asked without asking and dreamed without voicing their wishes.

Though their prayers were answered, none of us realized what they had received. Their father and husband returned home. His life was spared. Their God answered their prayers, but none of them knew the man who returned home. Was anything still the same back in the new Maxwell house? Home again, so much of me didn't return with me.

I felt marked. As Annie Dillard writes, I didn't know what the mark meant: "The sign on my body could have been an emblem or a stain, the keys to the kingdom or the mark of Cain. I never knew."[5]

I loved being home, but I did not know how difficult it would be. I did not know how many struggles awaited us. The next weeks and months brought those struggles. The keys and marks of my new self appeared as signs of our new times, scenes from our new motion picture. My wisdom seemed so small. My sons helped their father by reminding me of friends' names. *Could I not remember at all? Why did my brain seem so dead in particular places? Why could I not lead my sons as I had always wanted?* They led me and put up with me. I became angry quickly, as those who knew about this disease had predicted.

I learned about the disease. Not facts really; those I read and heard I could not remember. Instead, I learned about how I would live with the disease. I knew how odd my inner activity seemed, how different from anything ever in my life, in my body. My life's shift shook me. *Look to God,* I told myself. *Lean on Him. Let Him lead you. Learn from Him.* Proclaiming complete dependence on God *and* living it? I had believed it and hoped to apply it for so many years, but never before with that amount of energy. Tears rushed out like storms. Still, stress held on and wouldn't let go. I shook and slept.

Deep inside, I wanted to grow in God. He had saved my soul. Now he had saved my life. How much brain He would restore I knew not then; I know not now. *Still,* I thought, *He is God. He is. He is. I can live like this, just like this, with God helping me through. So many others live so long with so much worse. Why do I think I must receive so much more?*

So I prayed for help. I prayed for God to improve my focus. For God to deal with my frustration. For God to free me, if not from the pain, at least from the pain I brought others through my behavior. I knew I needed to please God. I continued praying, always finishing with the same two words: *Please, God.* Begging Him, I longed for help. I asked so often, with tears and fears near, with hopes and dreams and faith seeming to grow. Today? *Pray,* I told myself. Tomorrow? *Pray,* I told myself. I did and asked God *please.*

I talked too much. Is that why Debbie and Cecele Brocato always left together for another room? Cecele visited three times a day to work on my healing with acyclovir, a strong antibiotic. She laughed and prayed with us. She said we blessed her. No question, she blessed us. Deb needed a friend like her.

Cecele came to complete a cure for the man who could not remember her name. Did I make sense when I talked? What did she and Debbie say when they entered the other room?

Debbie doesn't answer that question, but she remembers: "You left the hospital with a pic line still in and a home care nurse coming to do your IV. She was from Jackson, Mississippi, and you ministered to her even in your weak state."

*****

Most people wonder about future events, opportunities, and experiences. We deal with doubts and dreams. Hopes may hide inside the clouds of questions. And faith may shift, however slightly. It can also make a different, better change. Maybe stiffen, maybe subtract the artificial additions to religion, to reality, to renewal. That shift could and would come in me, I trusted. That ambition, my wonder, and my wanting.

For me, the radical physical change had occurred without a warning. In the same way, spiritual disasters lead to eternal sickness, and yes, we have been cautioned. This event alerted me—though I knew truth, preached truth, wrote truth, tried to live truth—about the whole truth. Not of today only, but of tomorrow. The truth of tomorrow. Home again, staring at a new life, I could learn much about living the truth as my family cared.

Years ago—though I seem so small again now, it was years ago when I was young—I surrendered to God through Jesus. Since then, in other prayerful moments, I have yielded more deeply. Isn't that normal? Growing, slowing, picking up speed again? Spiritually, it seems normal to move from tension to wonder. From success to failure. From self-worship and condemnation to salvation and freedom.

Why pretend? The context of life, real life, eternal life, can keep us focused whether or not we can see. It keeps us listening, whether or not we can hear. Moving forward, whether or not we can walk or run or ride or fly. During this season, some of my focus made a quick switch. Though my mind could not think correctly, my spirit believed Jesus was right: Dying to self leads to life, and our Maker expresses His power when we cannot possess any more power in ourselves.

I knew that. Some moments I caught on; other times, circumstances crushed me. I kept trying, though, to know that.

From sermon lessons I preached for years to a sickness lesson I faced for myself. For God? Words that had grown too familiar now made more sense than ever: "My grace is sufficient for you, for my power is made perfect in weakness."

I asked for help.

***

Since I could not begin preaching in person yet, our church business administrator, Les Hall, worked out phone calls to me so I could communicate with my church. I thanked them. They listened to me. They had prayed but had not understood. They did not know what would happen next. Only God did. So we talked, listened; talked, listened. We cried, prayed, smiled, and hoped.

A phone call in faith, praying for a future of better moments. For what would come tomorrow. Questions and answers in minds mixed with dreams or doubts. About tomorrow.

For now, care for one another was what I had preached before. I did not speak it to force their love and tenderness upon me. Then, though. Then, when I needed it more than I even knew, they cared for me.

Would I still speak to them? Would I return? Not knowing, we talked, listened. That is all we could do then.

***

Think of how many moments we miss. We focus on an obstacle instead of viewing it as an opportunity. Evangel Assembly could have dismantled. They could have entered power struggles. Or they could have lived out true Christianity. True love does that. And I am grateful; their true love succeeded.

A few years ago, a pastor told me his disappointing story. His congregation had not accepted the new man an illness forced him to become. No caring. No true compassion. His lack of faith had caused it all, they assumed. Maybe, some thought, a hidden sin should be blamed for his illness.

He changed careers and later asked me, "How did your church walk with you through your struggle?" I'm not sure how I answered, because I'm not sure how they did it. But I'm sure of this: Church should be a family affair, not a war zone or a power struggle. A family of unique but related team players who do what is best for one another and for the building of His Kingdom. Isn't that it? Isn't that what Jesus expects of His body?

For better and for worse. When rich or when poor. In sickness and in health. Until death shall part us. Debbie had stated similar vows when we were married. My boys hadn't voiced such phrases, but their commitment was expected. They lived out unspoken vows, even during the worse and poor and sickness seasons.

Some in our congregation couldn't take it. They left when we needed them the most. But I can't be angry. I could hardly take it myself.

How shall God show His love? Would He choose to take sinful, selfish people and buy them for His own? Would He then decide to allow them to display His love by caring for one another?

It doesn't sound like a successful tactic for taking over the world, but it is God's plan. Placing messed-up people all together and telling them to love one another; telling the healthy to love the sick; informing the happy to hold the sad; instructing the wealthy to support the poor—what a strange strategy! I don't think God would get elected to office.

But I saw His plan in action.

I read many words from many people over the next few months. The letters typed and the cards mailed resembled to me the signature of God, the assurance that I was not alone.

The cards stayed close to my bed in an organized array. In the order I wanted. After all, each reminder helped me remember. Debbie read them to me at first; I reread them slowly when I began to read again. A few broadcast schemes for quick healings, but most showed true care. Their kind confessions calmed me and shifted my thoughts from my weakness to God's strength.

My sister Laura and Susan, a friend from our church, sent cards daily. For weeks, for months. Neither missed a day of humor and kindness on paper. Both knew what to say, what scenes to display, what prayers to pray. Their cards stopped coming on the same day. It wasn't planned. Susan and Laura ended their daily routine. Together, though separated by states and miles, they had started, continued, and stopped in sequence. I was surprised, but it was time.

That is how God is. That is how we are.

People in need of people, and people who respond to God's call. That is how God works.

I do thank God I didn't have to take it alone. Most of the people in our congregation came along for the ride. A collection of people. A family at home, a family so large, a spiritual family. That was us.

6

Your Love Broke Through

In the actions of countless normal people, His love broke through, affirming His presence with me. When we are uncertain of His love or presence, He sends people to remind us.

My lunches with Jim George offered therapy that showed God's love. Were our lunches strange for Jim? I cried so often. He told me to not lose my temper. He told me to talk nice to my wife. I couldn't understand my emotions; I couldn't stop the tears.

Jim cared. Meals tasted good, but that is not why our restaurant became a favorite. I needed the privacy. A hideaway of calmness where only a few people could hear me as I talked and talked, cried and cried. Jim stayed with me. He helped me order my spaghetti, kept me calm, and helped me believe again. Cecil Murphey described what Jim did this way: "To those who are too weary to go on, we can wrap our arms around them and say, 'Let's go together.'"[6] People. God sends people.

The caregiving I received appears weird from the perspective of people who despise Christians and argue that none live their doctrine. I want everyone to know that many people seek to live what they believe. Many friends wrapped their arms around us and displayed acts of kindness. They took us to eat or brought food. Dave and Amy Welday went to lunch with us. And cards kept coming. Prayer cards came, as churches around the world listed me among those needing God's help. Lee Grady called often during my bad moments.

Dianne Chambers, my other secretary, listened to me, watched me cry, helped me spell, reminded me of words. Through each weakness, she brought strength. I needed so much help. She didn't mind.

I hated forgetting names I had known for so long. I wrote, *Unique pain to me. Not pleasant. Good in the long run? I shall see. He shall see. My God, that is who. He can turn the painful into peaceful, pleasant growth. We doubt it. We struggle to see it. He can do it. I prayed with my dear friends that He would do it for me through this crazy time. This time I hated.*

God sent people to go with me. Garrett and I attended Emmanuel College together. He came from Virginia; I lived near the school in Franklin Springs, Georgia. We now wish we had built the friendship before our senior year. A few professors were probably glad we didn't. Regardless, we made up for lost time. He often visited us in Orlando before making this town his town. Many years ago, he came to help us get a church started. Now Garrett lives here, is married, and, as always, makes a difference in my life.

He especially made a difference when I returned home from the hospital. Debbie attended college weekly to maintain her teaching degree. During her absence came Garrett's presence. So different from our past time together, we experienced new fellowship. I talked often, making sense some of the time. Garrett listened often, which remains his gift. God knew Garrett could simply be there for me. He was. I thanked God and Garrett.

Debbie and my sons thanked Garrett too. He took their side and worked with my son Taylor, rebuking my attempt at driving long before I was legally allowed to drive again. When I stole keys and drove less than a mile, they turned against me because they cared. Harsh rebukes spoke in love. I remember. Why can't I pick and choose what to forget?

Garrett listed my humorous words during my stay at the hospital. It added smiles during the strange time. He knows me well enough to guess what my thoughtless brain may have thought if it could have. Here is his top ten list:

*TOP TEN THINGS SAID IN AND AROUND
CHRIS' HOSPITAL ROOM:*

10. "Will the insurance pay for all this?"
9. "I guess the compliments gave him the big head."
8. "Is there a newspaper in there?"
7. "Won't any of these machines pick up WMMO?"
6. "This is going to make a great sermon illustration."
5. "I hope they don't have to cut my hair for anything."
4. "Can I stay in here until Georgia Tech loses?"
3. "No, we can't get an oatmeal cake into an I.V."
2. "No, you can't choose who gives you a sponge bath."
1. "Don't tell anyone I'm really in here for a hair transplant."

Family and friends needed his humor. Later, when understanding returned, I laughed. It did good like a medicine.

Garrett can be too quiet at times. But he can also add funny words just when we need them. He is real. I like that. He is also the kind of person you can be real around. Not demanding perfection, he accepts people. I am, fortunately, one of those imperfect people he accepts.

People. God sends people.

Janice Combs also faced difficulty while serving her God. Her medical wisdom explained my MRI results to me; her faith reminded me that God does not depart from His people. She knew the seriousness of my illness. Her view of my difficulty also showed how praying and hoping make a difference. Her view of my life lifted me and reminded me of a Great God. Janice wrote this not long after my struggle:

Throughout years of a difficult marriage and a heartbreaking divorce, Chris stood by me as a tower of strength, encouraging, praying, counseling, and crying with me. He was always there, responding to the prompting of the Holy Spirit to call when I needed to hear that someone cared.

How could my tower of strength crumble physically and mentally? I was awed by his intellectual capacity and skill as an orator. Now he could barely communicate. I went from shock and disbelief to incredible sadness and a tremendous feeling of loss.

I knew if Chris couldn't be Chris totally, it would be like torture for him, and he would not fight to live, which is essential to conquering a critical illness. It broke my heart when I felt that Chris didn't know me. He had stood by me through my life's darkest moments. Now I thought I was a stranger to him. I wanted to comfort him as he had done so many times for me and say, "It will be okay because God is in control."

I am thankful God answered our prayers for Chris. His recovery is a miracle. God is faithful to walk with us through the darkest valleys of our lives. I learned that truth from Chris before his illness. Now others will learn from his example.

So many of her thoughts refuse to leave my mind. I think about them and ask questions. How are we now responding when people need to know someone really cares? How many people hear us say "I love you" and also know with certainty that we mean what we are saying? If our strengths depart and our gifts disappear, what is left?

Janice is correct about God's faithfulness. He doesn't depart. I knew that truth before this happened to me. I know it now in new ways, in an awareness that my confident former self could not fathom.

People. God sends people.

After my illness, I listened to tapes of sermons people preached in my stead when I stayed in the hospital or home. Les and Dianne Hall were such a blessing. Les and Dianne, personally and congregationally, had to deal with the strangeness of the moments. Gifted by God, they amazed me and kept things going. They listened to me talk, watched me cry, listened to me talk more, more, more. They helped answer my many questions. They told me the names of my friends, names I could not remember.

That first Sunday flooded Les with stress, yet his sermon brought powerful thoughts to the congregation. His own uncertainty joined with a deep belief in God. His hope for my improvement linked with his conviction that each person needed to grow spiritually. He voiced his honest challenge.

The congregation prayed for me with sounds of sadness and hope.

I wrote about them in my journal: *Les and Dianne sat in difficult positions. Since they came to the church I pastored, they blessed me regularly. Christ's love came through their attitudes of servanthood. Their past hurts had clothed them with a kindness needed within God's care. God used them greatly during my sickness. He continued to shine through them.*

While I was in the hospital, they helped Deb, the church, and the sick man. After that, this time now, this uncertain time that has improved and stopped and improved and stopped, during this time they continue helping me. The word or name I cannot remember, they know. My situation, they are patient. Amazing.

Dianne also wrote about me, offering her perspective of those events and challenging me to live on as the man God saved. Les and Dianne now serve at Youth With a Mission in Colorado Springs, but I'll never forget their example of Christian care. Her words remind me of so much:

March 1996 will be a month long remembered. When the call came from Debbie that she was taking you to the hospital, it was total shock. You were never sick, or if you were, you would never admit it to anyone. When we arrived at the hospital and were allowed to see you for a few minutes, I couldn't believe how sick you looked and sounded. And I felt like Deb was at a loss about what to do.

After the diagnosis and the long days and nights of staying at the hospital and seeing you out of your head and not knowing what to do, it was very frustrating. You were always in control, always knew exactly what you wanted to do, and now you didn't know up from down, left from right, my name.

I wanted to take all the pain away and all the fear I felt Deb had, but could do nothing but be there for you.

As you improved, it was a different frustration. I never knew when to help and when to just let you try to get out what you wanted to say. You had always been too independent. It was extremely difficult, and still is, for you to accept help from others. I'm still not sure when to supply a word for you, or when you want to figure it out for yourself.

I feel God did not cause all of this, but He has allowed some amazing things to happen as a result. I have seen a tenderness and compassion in you I never saw before. You always had concern for your flock, but not like now. I also believe, on the other hand, that you do not put up with as much junk. Life is too precious and short to waste our time on petty little things. I've learned through your illness that we never know what tomorrow holds.

I think others have learned you are not the answer they need; God is. It was hard on some to adjust to the fact that you were not there all the time they wanted someone to cry on. They had to go to God instead, and I believe that was a blessing in disguise.

I have seen you become bold speaking to others about God in a way like never before. How refreshing. I also think because of the struggles you face daily with trying to remember words and other things, that you understand the frustration some of us feel when we know we should do something, but just can't get it done in ourselves. I am learning from you and what I see in you, that it is okay to ask for help.

God has used you mightily through all of this. And the things you see in yourself as shortcomings, we, your flock, see as being human, not perfect. Yes, you feel inadequate; join the club; so do we, but thank God we don't have to live on our adequacies, only God's in us.

Thanks for your example of hanging in there.

Made a difference? I might not know much, but I do know this. Prayer does make a difference. Why would God invite us to ask if He did not plan to respond? Dianne, Les, and our church family stayed firm for Debbie and my family to lean on during that unexpected time.

7

Lean on Me

Did you notice Dianne's words? *Frustration. Struggle. Fighting to exist. Hanging in there.* I notice those words as I reread them. They remind me of what makes endurance possible.

As believers, we choose to live while "leaning on the everlasting arms." But we often wonder about the form of those arms. Are they muscular in appearance? Are they always just the right temperature and touch? Or can they be our least favorite color and come to let us lean on them at the most inconvenient time? Have we ever thought His hands might be our hands, His arms our arms?

The apostle Paul used this analogy about the group of people sharing his beliefs. He labeled them as individual body parts and the corporate tribe as the body. He argued that no member of the body was just like any other. Uniqueness came for a purpose. Each part is important for the health of the whole body. Sounds both creative and logical to me. My seasons of leaning helped me learn more truth of that imagery.

As a pastor, I don't like the CEO approach. I'm more of a "let's all agree, give a few high fives, pray together, and always love one another" kind of leader. I want others to do their thing, me to do my thing, and all of us do those things for the good of the whole. The best lesson I taught and the best theory I learned both came from the same class: Chris' Sickness 101. Though I failed many of the tests and neglected many of the assignments, I learned about allowing others to engage in my life.

They also learned to learn from a not-so-brilliant leader. By relating to and welcoming such a leader, a tribe can grow in strength. By assisting and accommodating such a captain, a team can grasp the crucial value of every position. I needed helpers to help and leaders to lead; fortunately, most of the members gathered together in spirit and in truth, playing to win.

I'm not called to hide away in a monastery. I'm not expected to live in isolation. I'm commanded by my Coach to play my position on the team. Even during a stay on the injured reserve list, I could find ways to help the team win. Many teammates worked to help me win.

What did they do?

They mowed our grass. They cut my hair, which, back then, was very long. They came over to read, to cook, to clean, to pray. They drove me to my appointments while I probably drove them crazy. They cooked food, bought food, served food, ate food—all while knowing that Chris was still extremely picky. They fussed at me when I disobeyed doctor's orders. They cried when I cried. They tried to laugh when I tried to tell jokes. They helped me learn to read and remember.

What did they do?

They lived out their faith. While mass-market madness informs us about the failures of church people, can't this brain-damaged man stand up and shout to the world? Can't I proclaim what I have experienced? I want to stand up and speak up: "Jesus loves me, this I know. Those who trust Him showed me so."

This little one felt I belonged to Him because of them. Though so weak, strong friends shared the muscle. A phone call can change a mind. A hug can change a heart. A smile can change a world. My mind and my heart and my world were changed. One person at a time: sweet Jesus.

Though the Halls are now working for a missions organization, my other Dianne is still on staff. And I still ask a lot of questions. Dianne Chambers, now Evangel's office administrator, recently saw the expression on my face. It warned her that she was about to be asked a serious question. She knew the old me, and she knows the new me. Being on staff, she knows much about my struggle to know. I asked Dianne, "What do you remember from eight years ago?" Instead of requesting a verbal response, I asked Dianne to e-mail her thoughts to me. She did. And she did remember.

I remember being in the office, answering what seemed like a thousand phone calls, and longing to know how you were doing. I remember not being allowed to go to the hospital to see you, and not having the confidence to do it anyway. I remember going to a Ladies' Night Out and having everyone there ask me how you were doing. I remember explaining to them that no one was allowed to visit you. I remember being so worried about you and just wanting to see you and trying to be encouraging for everyone who was calling into the office. I remember one of the ladies in our congregation coming into the office to help me answer all the phone calls we were getting from people wanting to know about you. We finally put a message on the answering machine with updates about you because we could not handle the volume of calls. I also remember one person who would call the same time each week to get an update on how you were. So many were so worried about you. I remember finally being allowed to go see you in the hospital and taking you a big chocolate chip cookie to eat. I remember being so relieved and grateful when you knew me, even though you didn't know my name! That's what I remember.

What do I really remember?

What am I really doing now to listen better, to care more, to show many more people how they are loved? How many times have I forgotten more than names?

If I lean on Him, they can lean on me. If I lean on them, I am leaning on Him.

It is His Body, the church. Imperfect, sick people all agreeing about real life. I pray I lean on that.

8

Every Life's a Story

The illness had hit me the first week of March 1996. As the new Chris entered a new May, I met a new friend. Patti began working on me.

She asked questions during visit number one. If I couldn't answer, Deb could. The new me needed help and helpers to help with the help. Out of control, I talked—often too much. And I cried—much too often. During our first meeting, then the next, my eyes let moisture rain frequently around Patti. She stared at my laughing and my talking, my learning and my anger. Mondays and Wednesdays and Fridays, from 1:00 to 2:00, Patti worked on me for eight weeks.

The former me had played softball near her office, met friends near her office, eaten meals near her office. The new me met Patti *in* her office. And she had to be the one in charge.

The former me helped people and made them smile. They cried while I encouraged and hugged and loved. Then? A role reversal. Then? The trouble's location stared back as I glanced in a mirror. Then? The new me was the patient, and Patti was the leader; she needed to work with me, work on me, work me, work me.

In my journal, I called my speech therapy a one-on-one match that Patti was determined to win. That was, then, the only way I could also win.

I asked, "Will I ever help others again? Will I always need help like this?" Patti steered my questions in new directions, guiding me toward recovery. Her face displayed calm control. The glasses covered her cautious eyes; her smile was often forced; the smell in the room reminded me of kindergarten. We talked about past and future, but we lived in the present, tackling a noun or a question, testing a thought, tossing noise and silence in our brief moments on a planet I had never landed on before.

She showed patience for my tears and my lengthy stories. She also kept me from touring too far off course. Her course, of course. "Let's get back to my question," Patti usually said as she sat straight and tilted her head.

Her brief, appropriate patience ruled; it was okay. Patti cared enough to live in reality. Her helper helped, learning facts and guiding procedures and teaming with Patti to keep me in the flow. Together they laughed at my jokes and lifted my sadness while dealing with my changed brain. They hoped to help me learn how to learn again. And live again.

Testing. Encouraging. Challenging. Reminding. Asking. Smiling. Shifting. Living. Questions and answers from Patti led me and lifted me higher from my low land. She kept me going. My gifts of speaking and writing needed and heeded her work on my weak mind. Her work flavored by consistency and care, Patti worked on me through more than a job. She carried concern. Her hopes for me became a part of me.

Did Patti know God walked and talked through her? Did she know?

Encephalitis leaves a person more emotional. It weakens mental ability. A Patti helps by luring patients toward appropriate rehabilitation. I should use an adverb in that previous sentence: *slowly*. Their work can slowly guide patients toward recovery. The slow part is the hardest part. For patients, for families, for Pattis. It was for me. I didn't like crying so much. I didn't like being unable to answer simple questions. I didn't like failing to repeat phrases stated to me only seven seconds before.

Hard work hits within our hearts when, as adults, we wish to grasp words our children know. As my former knowledge left home, my new life hurt my new self. No warning prepared me. Then, though, Patti came for rescue and recovery.

Patti didn't know me when I spoke or wrote before. She only met me when I cried, when I spoke large sentences in search of a missing word. Did she wonder if I spoke this poorly before?

She explained truth to me. Carefully, she asked questions and offered orders. Her questions allowed her to locate me. They let her test me when I smiled and cried and worked to remember a moment, a name, a noun. They fit our mix of mystery as I felt frustrated when improvements on a Monday disappeared by Wednesday.

Patti learned about my interests, and asked about sports to change my mood. I gave quick answers in segments and in sequence when she guided my thoughts into words hiding in my remodeled mind. Those brief question-and-answer fragments nudged me toward thinking and flowing, toward recalling and knowing. Sometimes it worked. Patti learned about basketball while reminding me of my memories. Sometimes.

With Patti, I worked. And I laughed. With me, Patti worked. She also laughed.

Her work was very good. Because of her I am better.

***

I often think about how many Pattis venture our way. We could learn from them. They could help us when pride or doubt or self-talk get in the way. Like they tried to for me, those ingredients spoil a perfect match. If they are thrown out and released, we can make room to receive help.

What did Patti learn from serving as my therapist, my helper, my protector? I wanted to know so I could know more. Seven years after the event, I interviewed my helper:

What was I like when you first saw me?

"Very kind, but very confused and frustrated. You were frightened with all the sudden changes. You didn't like being uncertain over what would happen next. We started testing to find out where you were; then we focused a lot on your memory and retrieval."

How did I compare to other patients with similar damage?

"I've seen people who were more impaired and people who were less impaired with similar injuries. In your favor was that you were so young, so motivated and had such a tremendous support system."

I like you calling me young and motivated. But tell me more. Was I really stubborn?

"Yes. Let's call it motivated; you were definitely not going to be stopped. You had a strong support system to find ways of working around the problems. It made a big difference that you already had people helping you develop some fantastic *convincitory* strategy. It is a lot harder for those recovering by themselves. Some also refuse to accept where they are."

What was it like for you when my mind wanted to go in different directions?

"Your attention struggled. That, combined with the amount of concentration it took for you to come up with your thoughts and express those thoughts; it wasn't easy for you. As you were thinking, a word would trigger, and you would shift to that idea, then another idea. It was tangential; you would just wander around. I would have a key word or a topic on the table to help you refocus about what we were talking about."

We are talking about my early days of recovery. Why does my mind still do that? Is it a permanent problem?

"To a certain extent, yes. But you're so much more aware of it now. You can catch it coming. Even early on, when you started preaching again, you had your support system giving you people to read for you. A lot of the gains weren't because of what I was doing, but because of what you were doing, and what the Lord was doing. I've done similar things with others, but the outcome wasn't as successful. It is a team effort."

We paused for a few moments while Patti fed her mother. We prayed and laughed until we both were ready to continue.

"Part of the emotionality is caused by the injury. You aren't always able to control things. Plus, adjusting to the many changes of your life. You are labile. People battle that in different ways, like emotional extremes or blood pressure changes, etc. When you were full of joy, all of a sudden your emotions shifted to another extreme. It triggered responses. Kids seeing Dad change like that isn't easy. People often get too scary because of being scared. It was challenging. But at times you were very funny. You tried so hard."

Why did the insurance stop my recovery? How could they think I was truly functional?

"To me, functional is not getting up and getting dressed, but a patient doing what he or she did before in their environment. Insurance companies view the patient as not needing more therapy."

Is there anything positive to that?

"It also forces a patient to cut the rope and not be dependent."

I often think about going back to my school days. How different would my IQ test be?

"Your IQ is still there, but the results would be different. So much depends on time. It takes you so long. You also have side effects of seizures and medication."

I think I know what she means. My mind takes unexpected turns. I thought about seizures and concentration, about memory and recall. Maybe the silence voiced my question to her.

"When you have seizures, you have small gaps of time when you aren't aware. Those around you might not be able to tell. Kids have seizures and struggle to learn because of what they miss. Sometimes I can tell with the eye contact, expressions, body posture. Maybe swallowing more. It's hard to catch."

What do you think about Chris Maxwell's future?

"Adapt as needs change. Technology to remind you keeps advancing. Palm device and other helpful technology. Learn what works best for you."

Then, as we did in our early days, our roles shifted. Patti asked the questions. "What do you remember about those days?"

I told her what I remembered, that I resented my weaknesses, my endless search for a phrase to voice, my dependence on writing in my own world rather than facing faces while talking and teaching. I told her what still hadn't changed.

She knows I like illustrations and images. She said, "I had a mechanic as a client who told me it felt like the gears were spinning, but they weren't meshing; they weren't connecting to get things to really lock in place and function. He also struggles with finding the word he wants and holding onto it long enough to get it out. He wishes he could trap a word long enough to get it out."

Her phrase, quoting his phrase, grabbed my attention. I wrote it in my Palm. I join in his wishes to trap a word, to trap a word, to trap a word. At least long enough to get it out.

"Drawing helped your visualization. Now don't try to over-achieve. Change is hard to accept. But there are positives. You are calmer, but still motivated and creative. You're such a giving person. You learn the balance for yourself."

Express those thoughts? Takes so long? Gears spinning? Trap a word? Learn the balance? How do we all just wander around? What is God's key word or a topic on the table to help us refocus?

What would Patti say to you? Consider a few words worth remembering. Confused. Frustrated. Frightened. Finding a focus. All people battle weaknesses. We all, though, can find ways to face our facts and improve ourselves. Are you aware of your own battles? Are you adapting and adjusting, or denying and refusing to refocus?

Let's be motivated. Let's find a strategic support team and apply stubbornness in appropriate ways. When we wander, let's refocus. When we become aware of weaknesses, let's accept help.

Adjusting to change. Cutting ropes. Adapting.

As our gears spin but don't mesh, a Patti and a prayer can begin working on us.

And not just Mondays and Wednesdays and Fridays, from 1:00 to 2:00.

9

In a New York Minute

S ince my insurance company offered no more coverage for therapy, I could not return to Patti. Debbie wanted me to get more help, so Patti referred us to the Department of Communicative Disorders at the University of Central Florida.

Therapists at the University evaluated, assessed, tricked, trained, and drilled my removal of skills. My first test revealed weaknesses. They agreed to help. Their assessment? *Mr. Maxwell demonstrated mild anomic aphasia marked by semantic paraphasias, word retrieval difficulty, reduced spelling ability, and difficulty taking on new information. Mr. Maxwell needs speech and language treatment to target these deficit areas."*

Chris and Jennifer guided me as I labored to recall their names. College students worked through the University of Central Florida facility for people like me. Led by a strong instructor, they consistently challenged, tested, asked, and directed me. We spent weeks working together.

I improved, or so they said. Some days, some seconds, some sentences, I believed them. Other moments I felt so stupid—is that the word that fits here? I can think of no better term for that time and that type of emotional wondering.

My second test score showed much progress. Their comments honestly admitted in an official way what I felt regularly. I was getting better, but I was not where I had been.

Their two-paragraph conclusion of the second test hit the facts. One sentence, though, got most of my attention. I almost giggled as I read it: *Overall, Mr. Maxwell functions at a very high level, however often verbally expresses frustration with his memory deficits.*

Almost giggled.

Frustration? Me, frustrated? Of course, they wrote correctly. They listed many positives, thank God, but that issue hit me the hardest.

***

God knows what we need. He speaks that to us in so many different ways. If we let Him, He then helps bring improvement. I knew I needed His wonderful, amazing help.

Leaving Patti and finding new help in a new place was okay. Escapism runs from problems, avoiding reality, but wisdom and maturity realize that growth requires proper and painful changes, as well as accepting responsibility. Fighting through our addictions and assumptions, we can say yes when invited into a realm of change.

That fact wasn't easy for me to face. So much was so hard to face.

I share the feelings of Joni Eareckson Tada. She wrote, "I want to admit my weaknesses and not be discouraged by them. *And Lord, if I attempt things beyond my strength, may I always find help in You.* The healing is happening."[8]

To keep that healing and that dependence on God "happening," He often takes us where we have never gone before. Where we might be afraid to take the new us.

In November, six months after I came home from the hospital, Bob Williams and his family invited my family to go with them to New York City. I said no. Though I had never been to New York—had never expected to go, especially after changing so much—I couldn't imagine a friend paying our way. As often occurred with both the old and new me, I learned only slowly to change my mind. To subtract pride? To add the gratitude I always preached my listeners should live with? My turn?

Some things are so much easier to announce than accomplish, to counsel than apply. Humbling oneself ranks toward the top. Or the bottom.

It was my turn to humble myself and reply with gratitude. I said we could go, and we did—five Maxwells, five Williamses, and one huge New York City.

The cold Thanksgiving week warmed me. My thoughts traveled in reverse, searching for comparisons. I remembered again my early days of growing up in very small north Georgia towns. Orlando, my present dwelling, looks large to me. On our November trip, I visited a place larger than anything I had noticed before. Up close? Personal? There, feeling smaller than ever, I observed the larger. I felt as if I had been told not to be afraid, that I had found favor. I felt like a shepherd leaving his flock to follow the flow. I felt like a kid carried into a city. We were there.

Hearing about New York and watching news reports do not tell the full story. I thought being there could, would. Being there did. It wasn't only larger than I imagined. It was better. Friendly people, not hateful or rude. Real people, not creatures wearing masks and big city facades. Pretense kept a distance, or was it just my new mind? Scurry paused, or was it just my new time? Joy and hope housed there, not just hurry and hate, greed and jealousy.

The Williamses and the Maxwells in such a different world. God used a place and reminded me of Himself. His size. His wisdom. His power.

And I hoped they wouldn't have to remind me to take my medicine.

Ingredients tasted just right. My new life needed them more than I knew then. Plays, traffic, cold weather, honking horns, a parade I had seen only on a small screen eleven hundred miles away while my mother laughed or my grandmother cooked, meals and moments of reverent pausing: change. Closeness as a family. Closeness to another family. Closeness to strangers in a place so strange to me.

My year had hurled surprises my way, many unpleasant and painful. This disclosure heaved an endowment packed with holiday delight.

I never knew I would go there. I do not know if I'll return. Then and there, though, the city—all of it—was just what I needed.

Watching *Beauty and the Beast?* A reminder of motion: from sick to much better, from sad to glad, from insane to sane. Dramatic displays illustrated the realities of my life's stage. I spoke to myself in silence: *Few know what a beast I am now. I try to find beauty to hide it. To hide me. Will it heal me?*

Watching the parade? My interest in parades had marched away from me many years ago. I guess I tried to grow up, to get over what the little boy loved. There, controlled by cold air and a crowd of observers, my brain made me think it was working okay again. Images appeared; they were real displays of drama dressed for the season. Large and tiny creatures rushed and paused, sang and laughed. I felt the event parading into my vents, my veins, my cells, my soul. Maybe I should call it an awareness of my own march, my own masks, my own cold, my own child within. Maybe I should call it fun. Maybe it was okay to be young.

The good day became even better. Santa and his gang guided the first part at Radio City Music Hall's *Christmas Spectacular.*

Jesus ruled the remainder.

I admit, it shocked me. Not my brain's electrical system. The startle landed in my expectations of this world's entertainment. I stared in New York City, watching a dramatic display of what I consider the reason for the Christmas season. And my reason for still being alive.

Jesus. A name above all names? A name even I can remember? A name that found a way for God to forget my ugliness?

Jesus. I cried. I thought again of what I believe, and I considered my Savior, my Savior, my Savior. I glanced through a huge crowd observing an image of One who appeared to be observing us all. I thought of a Rescuer coming.

Jesus. My joy took a leap inside. I said one "hallelujah" a bit too loud. But no one seemed bothered. I wasn't bothered. I imagined being bathed again with clean water, framed again in life's big picture, roomed again with the star so often forced to remain behind our frozen, locked stages. The act of His coming out induced an unlocking and warming of my own stage.

God became a babe. Tiny and needy and new. Wrapped in swaddling clothes, lying in a manger. No room in the inn. No room in so many people and so many places today. I wanted to invite Him in me again. To ask for help from that tiny, needy, new baby because I felt so tiny, needy, and new. And naked. And old. And a baby. I wanted God to own me, to love me. I wanted my life to be His life.

Thanksgiving in New York City was Christmas for me. For us.

What else could I have hoped for? How else could each of us have been pleased?

I wanted my sons to stop asking for snow, even though I wanted it more than anyone else. I just knew too much. I had heard the weather report. It wouldn't come; the snow was to fall much farther north on that November night.

As we walked out of Radio City Music Hall, we couldn't explain the air. Pollution? Dust in the wind? No. I could hardly believe it: oh, me of little faith. Snow fell. Little white visitors slowly showing how hopes can drop our way. Snow fell. Like my sons and my friends, I cheered. Smiling, I hid my happy tears.

***

Snow continued falling as we walked back to the St. Moritz. A little snow, but snow. Cold weather, New York, great friends, life, family, holy drama, and snow: what a show. I thanked God. I thanked the Williamses.

The spectacle notified me that I had also become a babe. A formerly healthy man became tiny and needy and new. Wrapped in swaddling thoughts, lying in my damage and learning how to manage. I felt pummeled by this city's answers to questions I did not remember asking. Can't snow plummet when not in the forecast? Can't holiness descend into theatrical drama? Can't kindness emerge in busy cities? Can't friends find room for friends? If so, can't I still flow toward new cities and new seasons? Can't each of us—though so aware of weaknesses and rough edges, though so ensnared by scars and fears, though so crammed with the curses of voices informing us of forecasts and doubt—can't each of us believe there is room for all the babies who need a place of birth? Can't angels and songs and shining stars herald a story too holy to forget? Can't the tiny and needy and new us get wrapped again? Can't it snow?

All those questions prompted one big answer. Maybe the Weather Controller wants His sons and daughters to keep asking for the impossible. Maybe we need to look beyond weather reports and probable outcomes, even those predicted by doctors or CEOs or inner talk. Maybe we should just push away our doubt and self-control, board a plane, and say thanks. And wait for the wonderful.

Taking a risk. Daring the doubts. Noticing our needs. Looking for the holy in the midst of hype, the sacred in the city. Turning off the weather forecast, getting unlocked and warmed. Watching flurries fall. Receiving an invitation from a friend.

I felt a little Lord Jesus, a large Lord Jesus dare me and us to get ready for snow. He dares us every day. It might be our turn to get better than ever. After all, a Ruler can make good days even better, even spectacular, for the tiny and needy and new—me and you.

But show time might be delayed until we risk taking a trip.

10

When Love Takes You In

Ever ask God why things happen? I did. But I wasn't asking alone. Even those who refused to question God would take time to hold this pastor who did ask questions. Maybe they knew it could have been them.

It was about leaning on God, our Rock and Redeemer. Our Rescuer and Strength. Our Brain and Reminder. That was Him. That is Him.

The key? Leaning on those everlasting, ever loving arms. Leaning on Him.

It wasn't you who fought my battle. It wasn't you who struggled to accept a new Chris. But it could have been. Be honest; it could be any of us at any time.

Floyd Skloot writes with rhythm and rhyme; he writes poetic honesty. I like his confession:

I know it was nothing personal. I know I was simply a host the virus used to do the only thing it knew how to do, enact its sole pattern of growth. I was like a windowpane latticed with crystals of snow, simply present at the critical moment when the storm came along. From the virus' point of view, I could have been a stone, or a broth of monkey kidneys and Medium 199 as in the most sophisticated laboratory, a block of moss. Or I could have been you.[9]

As some heard the story of my sickness, they wanted to know more. They longed to glance at the effects of a storm of sickness. They chose to stare at my alive remains. They knew it could have been them.

Joe Coffey came to stare after he heard about my condition. Our relationship started with us as youth pastors playing against each other in basketball games. Our competitions on the court displayed his talent and leadership skills. We liked the same music and read the same books. When he saw a basketball in my car, heard Cockburn on my stereo, and noticed a Frederick Buechner book on my desk, Joe smiled. We began meeting to pray, ask questions and pursue true answers.

Then he moved up north. But distance did not separate our connections.

After hearing about my battle, Joe visited me, watching, listening to me cry. I needed him more than I knew. Did he know? God knew and made sure of it. I felt guilty that he came so far. He has no way to know how much he helped me spiritually and emotionally.

This time, we didn't shoot hoops. We talked, walked, prayed. I cried. I fussed. I talked, talked, talked. He listened, asked questions. He made a difference.

What did he think about it?

When I got the call from Debbie, I made arrangements to come down and visit. I wanted to see Chris—at least to hug him even if he didn't know my name.

He remembered much about our history together, but my name gave him trouble. His eyes were active and searching, alternatively showing confusion, recognition, and fear.

He would ramble—emotions flowed freely. I was struck by his faith, which was like a rope that held him suspended in a state of limbo. He knew enough to know that he had been swept off solid ground and was now without footing. He was equally aware of the rope that suspended him, although he had no idea whether his feet would ever touch down again.

It was not sad to see him. It was fascinating to see a man of God with nothing but God to cling to. He wept often. He cried because he could see his own life in a new light and he was convicted. He cried because God had given him eyes to see the suffering of others. He cried because the sheer goodness of life overwhelmed him. It was as if Chris was free to experience the reality and the force of both good and evil, and it swept

*him away like a flood. It frightened him and, at times, provided him
with an intense peace.*

Joe wrote about what he saw and what he learned. He
knew from watching someone struggling to be himself, to be
somebody, to be someone making sense out of words and life.

Others watched me. They kept watching and learning.

Now? I'm different from the new Chris that Joe came to
visit. But I'm still not the old Chris Joe played against and
prayed with so many years ago.

Now? I know so much about knowing less.

I still study to obtain information and to grasp my recovery,
my reality. Encephalitis. The cause of my effect of not knowing.
It surprises you. Like a hidden secret, it is difficult to discover.
Aphasia, another word I came to know well. "Because of injuries
or disease, weakness mentally to grasp or gather."

What a learning experience. New words. Illustrations. I
play games to track numbers, rules, or order. The poster at my
clinic gave this prophetic utterance: *An impairment of the power
to use or comprehend words, usually acquired as a result of a stroke, and
sometimes from head injury or brain tumor.* They needed my picture
beside it.

V. S. Ramachandran's words in *Phantoms in the Brain* mirrored
my thoughts: *Parts...had forever vanished, lost in patches of
permanently atrophied brain tissue.*[9]

Rebuke it? Or realize the new me needs to rejoice while
accepting life and learning again to live?

My battle with viral encephalitis had affected my left
temporal lobe. It caused deterioration of nerves within the
brain. My new weak points included language, learning, and
memory. A friend said, "He is more real, more sincere." How
can brain infection, abnormal electrical discharge of neurons,
and flaws in perception and memory make a man more real?
Good question.

Can pain bring long-term blessings? Can disabilities give
us the honor of allowing God, really allowing God, to do in
us and to us and through us what is impossible without His
Strength? Before my more-real-more-sincere change, I taught

the biblical truths of Joseph's disappointment becoming God's appointment, of David's size giving God a chance to show Himself, of Christ's death bringing beauty to all who are washed. I had taught it. This time, I think I caught it.

But I keep working to learn it and live it.

When I read about mild traumatic brain injuries (MTBI), I need verbs for more than the past, which deal with the cause. Verbs for present and future problems can define, warn, and explain the days to come. And my days, my many days, did come. I'm glad others knew about my not knowing:

"An MTBI is experienced as a personal disaster. If your injury has robbed you of some of your ability to function at work or at home, this can have a crushing effect....You may feel less able to interact....After an MTBI, you have to face the possibility that you will never be as you once were. This experience constitutes a loss of self, and a loss of self triggers grieving."[10]

In the book *Coping With Mild Traumatic Brain Injury*, the authors suggest an awareness of what to expect from an MTBI: denial of the loss, anger, bargaining, disorganization, despair, depression, acceptance or resolution. I label the sequences as seasons of sadness. I worked to endure each episode by merging in a little gladness. Often, I could not find it. But often, it found me. Even as I cried and questioned and hoped to develop my adjustment to life, I sought a joy to inundate every portion of the recovery and acceptance.

They also write, "Working through and letting go of grief is difficult, but it can be made less so by redirecting your energy to such activities as learning new skills, volunteering your services, or being a point person for another brain-damaged individual."[11] I love quotes like that, which justify and validate my desire to do and do and do. I also like to know I'm not alone in not knowing, in change, in disappointment. I pray I also remember these words even if I can't memorize them: "Withdraw your emotional investment in the person you once were in order to move forward with your life. Realize that the person you are today is not a poor substitute, but a composite of your old and newly acquired selves."[12]

They call it "learning to let go." I think of words like *release, surrender,* and *forgive.* They differ from *quit, give up,* and *resign.* I worked to make the new me a successful me. But I also realized that each person struggles to release, surrender, and forgive. As I worked to adjust, I prayed for our God to help each of us refuse to live addicted to our former selves and to motivate us to move forward toward newness, change, and transformation.

Mary Dement noticed my change and adjustment. She showed me a letter she wrote to a friend, asking me if her facts were correct. Would I know? Her note told me more than I knew.

How is my church? Thanks for asking. On March 6, 1996, Chris went to the emergency room. He was in really bad shape. He had a major headache and then passed out. He was saying odd things. After numerous tests, they diagnosed him with encephalitis. He was in intensive/critical care for a long time.

It is the strangest thing I've ever seen in my life. He can't remember names, words, etc. It's like the "name file" on the computer of his brain has been deleted. He would know YOU if he saw you. He would remember who you were and that you are my friend. He just wouldn't be able to remember your name.

He is doing much better now, although still having memory problems. God has really touched him and our congregation through his illness. He is preaching. There is such humility to him now. It's been interesting. Be praying.

Remembers this but not that. Files deleted. Knowing a person and not knowing the name. Doing much better but still having problems. Memory problems. God has touched?

God touched, Mary wrote, both me and our congregation. How should we label such a touch? Violence? Wrath? Or a Sovereign being aware of what occurs and protecting me from worse damage? A true Lover knowing and showing that love through rescue and recovery?

I leaned on Him and the people in our congregation. Learning while leaning, I lived again.

11

We May Never Pass This Way Again

Debbie's Christmas card informed family and friends about our life—our *new* life. It also allowed her to disclose how rough the year had been. She didn't present a full broadcast of her pain, but her comments revealed more than she knew about our difficult year.

Dear Friends and Family,

This is just an update on our year. As most of you know, our year was going rather smoothly until March, when Chris was diagnosed with encephalitis. God has been more than gracious. Chris has come a very long way but still has a ways to go. The doctor says it may be another year before he is back to normal, if ever. Please continue to pray for him. He continues to have trouble remembering names and nouns and must rest a lot. The good news is he is reading, writing, spelling, preaching, and back to work full time now. He is also back to coaching Aaron's basketball team, though not quite up to coaching the other two guys' teams yet.

After writing about our sons' ages and activities, she added, *They have had their ups and downs with Chris' illness, but they are learning firsthand of God's faithfulness.*

Deb informed our friends about the cause and effect, about sons racing in age, about a dog, about school, about a husband driving again. It was nice of her not to mention my driving the whole family crazy. She did write, though, about God's faithfulness.

The next fall Deb began teaching at a private school. The shift from home school gave the guys another class to pass—another one about life's changes. They could again implant God's faithfulness. Their questions and doubts and fears could find help from the true source of care.

I looked at the ages of our sons as I read Debbie's confession. And I look at them now—their ages, their faces, their thoughts, their real beings. I notice the march from that note to this journal, from their facial expressions then to their conversations now, from learning God's faithfulness then and still seeking to learn it, to live it, to love it. That search was, and is, a family affair.

My mind helps me remember in pieces how this family fared with my change. My journal held notes. My family took over, in hopes of informing me about myself.

I remember when the relatives invaded the privacy of my bedroom one evening after I had returned home from the hospital. They planned to tell me how bad I had become. Let's label it their "State of My Confusion" address. My father-in-law raised his voice and joined my sister Janet in working to help me notice the new man I had become. I argued, debated, and, eventually, was defeated. They were correct. The family knew the old me and the new me; they wanted me to hear their side of this story. After my initial outrage, I surrendered. None of us knew that "struggle" chose to find a home in our home, or that it found a dwelling place in my mind. From denial to despair to reality, I wrestled often and won. Because of care, it was a family affair.

Mark Rutland wrote, "God's willingness to help us must be met by our willingness to be helped."[13] Being willing to be helped gave me true help from those who truly cared.

When the holidays came, we visited Georgia to see family and friends. I had hoped all would go well—mainly my mind, my words, my emotions. Crying, I remembered childhood. I saw people. I spotted places. Events, individuals, groups, scenes, mistakes, questions, answers, surprises, habits, and hopes came to my mind. God loved me when I lived as a child.

Could I remember? I found that long-term memory functioned better, outperforming my short-term memory's efforts to place words to the world and names to the faces. It felt like a sport, flaunting a little competition.

Uncles reminded me of my mother. Sisters reminded me of myself, of our childhood together. They told me tales of time before. Their southern accents reminded me of my days before, of myself laboring to live and learn again. Christmas reminded me of my Friend, the Christ who kept me through the strangeness of this year, through it all my Master and King. I thought of Him while hearing people sing about His birthday.

Yes, my emotions and behavior had improved. Relatives realized their prayers were answered, but Chris still wasn't his old self. I remembered names of people from long ago better than the names of those who recently entered my life. During the holidays it seemed fine—maybe too fine. No place like home, they say. But which home? Now or then? I knew one truth for sure: My family and old friends had prayed for me. My visit didn't stop their prayers; what they saw, one told me later, encouraged them to continue praying. I was blessed by their endurance and by God's listening ear.

Another year. A new year. I remember how time races, passing us suddenly and leaving us shocked. Many of us feel old as we ask where it went.

My family and our congregation began those twelve new months by setting goals and making commitments. I started the year asking God for help, wanting Him to keep me close. Very close.

Jumping into new years, most of us think we know so much. We may plan weeks and months, days and hours, minutes and seconds, but we cannot plan for the surprises. Surprises scurried to us that December, but their fallout would not end with the year. They would stay, and they would also come in new ways every day of every year, causing new views of ourselves. How many? How bad?

Unplanned issues wait; surprises will come our way. What we do about those surprises determines our future. Blaming the unexpected suggests excuses, but we can find victory amid the surprises. An explanation ranks far above an excuse. Defining, rather than defending, enables victims to face facts and move forward.

God's goodness and guidance: those I knew. In *The Lion, the Witch, and the Wardrobe,* C. S. Lewis suggests, "God is not safe, but He is good." Trusting Him during the todays and tomorrows of hurried years gives hope. Circumstances will come and surprise us, but they do not need to destroy or defeat us. Sure of God's goodness and His guidance, packed with His peace, we can stare at each rapid year and say we are ready. The Bible gives us numerous examples of this kind of ruthless trust.

Noah obeyed God, built the strangest of all possible accommodations, and survived.

Stephen, as stones ended his life on earth, stared toward heaven and praised the One he spotted.

Paul and Silas sang praise tunes in a prison cell's debut as a concert hall.

In a new year, in the first January as a new me, how might I build an ark when I notice no clouds, or spot a smile when I feel my body won't last much longer, or sing a song when I see walls locking me where I'd rather not be?

Summarize it this way: God wants us to really trust Him.

As questions tick with the clock's sway, I pray I live sure of God being the One Who is Sure.

***

Sometime in late December, I asked my middle son, Aaron, what he wanted for the New Year. He thought. I waited. He takes questions so seriously. The silence caused me to reconsider my request. Do I ask too many questions?

"I want us to go back through this year again," he answered.

For the New Year he wanted to return to the ending year? I felt shocked. A year he did not like, a year none of us liked—he wanted it all over again? I asked him why.

Of course, Aaron had an answer. "Now that we know about your sickness, we know what will happen. Before you get bad off, we'll tell the doctors what's coming. They can fix you before you get messed up. Then the year would be different." He paused and said, "That is what I want, to go back."

Aaron wanted to go back through the year again and fix my mental engine before it broke down. He knew what to avoid; he dreamed of defeating a disaster and returning to his familiar life with his former father. Aaron and I knew we couldn't go back. But he meant what he said.

It was my turn to talk. "We have a new, a brand-new, a newer-than-ever, never-before-lived year. We enter it not knowing what awaits us. We cannot have last year again, Aaron, but we can learn from last year and face this year better than we have ever faced any year before."

I talked longer, telling Aaron things my mind needed to remember: Last year is over, though its results aren't; we can't return and correct the damage; by God's recovery we can lunge, or be plunged, into this New Year with the fitting perspective; let's thank God for how things are much better than they could be.

Aaron smiled. His silent expressions indicated belief, hope. His pain paused for a moment. He then changed the subject, ready for me to close our between-the-two-of-us sermon. I asked him to stop, to let us pray. He wasn't surprised.

After I finished, we smiled. Aaron changed the subject again. He appeared ready for a really new, and much different, New Year.

He wasn't alone.

Neither of us was alone.

12

Ride Like the Wind

The man spoke with honesty. Confessing what he could no longer do, describing how his gifts had departed, admitting new fears and weaknesses. His testimony proclaimed not peace but pain, pressure, depression.

"Why do I have to take this medicine?" he asked. Pausing, he waited before continuing. Neither of us answered his question. I kept walking, holding my cell phone, wondering what he would say next. My heart told me he needed ears, not another mouth. Ears to hear his admission; a heart to understand his hurt. Slowly, he talked again.

"I've prayed for many others and watched God miraculously heal them. It worked for them. Not me."

His name is known. His accomplishments have amazed people. Now he struggles to do what felt so simple before. Doubt and defeat appear housed nearby.

I encouraged him to release those hurts; I advised him to keep a journal and avoid denial or despair. He continues to meet with friends who accept the new man as he is.

And he talks to me. Why? Because of my counseling degree or my encouraging words? No. My talents or title didn't open his heart. My sickness did. When he heard me speak about a life-changing experience, he felt I would relate.

That's the way my life is now. As TV shows interviewed me and promoted my book, *Beggars Can Be Chosen*, what did they really want to know? About my brain damage, about how it feels to have seizures, about my MRI results, about my forgetfulness. I was not asked about how I've effectively maintained good relationships with my three sons or how I communicate consistently with my wife. Reporters and editors, pastors and congregations want to ask, Does it embarrass your sons when they regularly remind you of names? How do your wife and congregation feel when you pause in a sermon because you can't pronounce a simple, common phrase? What do people think when they call and hear, "No, the pastor isn't available now; he is resting"?

Years have passed since my illness changed me. Encephalitis, though, set in motion an ongoing changing. Those ten days in the hospital, months of therapy, a lifetime of tests and medicine, and now epilepsy, the "new me" is a man I did not prefer to be.

The former me had no trouble spelling. The new me thanks God for Spell Check.

This brain once had no trouble remembering names or memorizing Scripture. Now? Our members remind me of their names; my three sons repeat what their father forgets; my wife works to accept her new husband, who goes by the same name as the man she married.

Can I really know more by knowing less?

I still hear Dr. Hal Pineless saying, "You now have epilepsy." He's the same one who used humor to help me smile, saying, "Remember what Clint Eastwood says in the Dirty Harry movies: 'A man's got to know his limitations.'"

Isn't that word, *limitations*, a curse? How can I view it as a blessing? A divine calling, sincere desires to do good, and inner longings to succeed all urge me to hide my limitations. So we pretend, acting as though we are not as we are. God works to change that.

We can all, in our own areas of sickness and weakness, relate to the apostle Paul. His story helps me face my limitations. Paul had things rough while remaining true to his divine Director. Even when I struggled to read, Paul's confession in 2 Corinthians 11:24-30 hit the headlines of my new mind: lashes five times, rods, stones, shipwrecks, swimming in the sea at night, on the move, in danger, needing sleep, starving, naked? I still work to join Paul, boasting of weaknesses and toasting the blessings of my mental limp.

While I was writing about my life-change, I asked Debbie to describe my illness to those who never knew the prior me. She talked with honesty. I thanked her as I typed and cried.

"This is my second marriage," she said. "God switched husbands on me in the fifteenth year of our marriage."

I later wanted, or thought I wanted, to know more. I asked Deb, "Describe your second husband."

"You have a totally different sense of humor," she said. "You go to bed early. We go to meetings in separate vehicles because I want to stay longer than you can. I need to fill in the blank and depend on my memory more because you forget so often. You have the most trouble remembering people's names. You are more emotional, crying more often than you ever did. It is difficult communicating."

Okay. I asked, "Is that all?"

"No," she answered. "You are not flexible at all about schedules."

Since writers need both pros and cons, since men need a little ego boost, and since I was desperate for at least one positive point, I pleaded for a more balanced synopsis. "Yes, there are some ways you are better. You're less inhibited; you are willing to say anything you feel you should say, but you say it carefully."

When blood flow, neural activity, and mental modification seem to labor in vain, what is occurring? Brain cells arrive at birth in a lifetime supply. Years after my illness, portions of brain remain permanently on pause. A word I expect to say transforms into an unrelated word before my mouth tosses it into the air. A name I said four sentences ago hides, refuses to allow me to locate it until I ask for help, feel embarrassed, and wonder why others think it is no big deal. Previously memorized Scripture keeps its distance.

I'm a different, unique me, and so much seems negative. But in search of "a more balanced" analysis, I ask myself, what are the real positives?

I previously taught a congregation to care, to use gifts, to serve. Then, during a season not planned or directed by our strategic visionary management, they got their chance. Many people applied those principles as I stuttered, struggled, and wondered why.

How do vanished parts of a pastor change a church?

My congregation knew Chris Maxwell. At least, the old me. Suddenly, without election or debate, they had a new pastor. Same name, same wife, same sons. The same, but completely different. This Chris cried daily, paused often, and struggled to remember. This teacher needed to be taught. PowerPoint presentations, Palm device dependence, no calls at certain times; my college professors never informed me that I would one day make radical changes for mere survival.

The church staff watched me weep, listened to me ramble, helped me spell, and reminded me of names, words, plans. My secretaries didn't just type and answer calls and copy. They tried to discern how to help. Ministers, leaders, parishioners, prayer warriors, and those who rushed away when their pastor lost his mind all helped by reminding me of reality. Sadness and confusion blended with acceptance; rejection stood beside *agape* love.

God had the medicine I needed. I still need it. I've finally learned to use this emotional madness in the river of gladness. Laughter really does good like a medicine (Proverbs 17:22).

Others mean well when telling me, "Oh, I forget all the time," or "I never could remember names," or "It's not your illness; you are just getting old." My face smiles, but my heart doesn't. I think, *Age didn't do this. It happened to a man in his thirties; it dove in quickly, altering everything.*

But instead of pouting, I joke. Maybe I again remember that story of my walk through hospital halls during the night of my "near-death experience," trailing tubes and preaching sermons no one understood when I wasn't, shall we say, dressed for the occasion. When I visited there before my illness, the hospital staff called me Reverend. After that midnight madness, they called me "the preacher with the cute butt." They still laugh.

When I think of that story, I forget for a moment about my
forgetting.

Naps? People from many countries let America's work-all-
day philosophy rob them of their traditional, midday Sabbath.
I have no choice. I fade, I shake, and I know. Those around me
know too: Chris' naptime. An honor? A privilege? When people
tell me they wish they had such an excuse, I want to shout,
"You do not want what I have." But they mean well. So I laugh.
And fall asleep for twenty-two minutes.

One night, my eyes opened, staring upward through the
dark toward our silent ceiling. The fan's rhythm and Debbie's
breathing provided a normal night. But I didn't feel normal,
not what had become normal to me. Something was different.
Me. I was different. At that moment, I woke into an awareness
of reality. Actually, I felt what we should choose to label as
normal. Normal, for the first time since my illness.

Pausing, I investigated my thoughts, my mind, myself. Was
I asleep, only dreaming of being awake and aware? Was I
imagining the experience of a complete healing of my damaged
brain? Was the electrical system inside my skull fully repaired
and now in use?

Names. Phone numbers. Passages of Scripture. Phrases from
my former self resurrected; I could remember.

I hit myself and found that I was truly awake. I hit myself
again to be sure. I decided to enjoy the moment and sat on the
side of the bed.

Wanting to wake Debbie and tell her the news, wanting to
march through the house and inform my sons, wanting to write
a book and preach a sermon to audiences waiting for a new me,
I avoided those desires. Praying and thinking and investigating
my mind, I thought. I could remember.

Questions clothed my curious mental conversation.
Searching and exploring previously damaged files, my working
mind worked and minded my instructions. Recalling a
memorized biblical text. Repeating a list of presidents in order
of election. Voicing names I had forgotten and nations I had
visited.

Words came in a calm, pleasant flow. The experience rushed, but paused. It hurried with strange composure, feeling like a life on water, floating softly though driven by a current of pleasure.

Glancing toward the clock, I thought, "Can I stop its movement and stay here forever?" I stood and walked. I prayed, while mingling intercession with the experience of remembering. Nouns and verbs. Numbers and events. Order and sequence.

I wrote a few notes to myself. Confession? Proof? Confirmation? To me, I needed to know that I knew. For me, I needed to remember how to remember.

After a return to the former mind of mine, I felt exhausted. Excitement left. I returned to sleep. I thanked God for the moment, the healing. I asked Him to let me wake again and still be healed.

The radio started at the set time, giving us the news and the weather as our wakeup call. I jumped from bed like it was an emergency. I saw my notes; it really had happened. I tested my mind quickly to inspect my thinking. It didn't take long to realize the true dream in the night chose to be a one-night stand. My electrical system's miracle at midnight did not wake with me. My healed brain had returned to its locked position inside a hemisphere hidden by my skull.

I thought about phone numbers and could not remember. About presidents and, after George Washington, I recalled only a few, and those in incorrect order. About verses of the Bible, and they had again been buried.

V. S. Ramachandran, in *Phantoms in the Brain*, presents an interesting argument regarding such nights, such moments, such experiences. I read his narratives and notice a portion of myself in those unrelated realities. As I've studied about damaged brains remembering again, or missing legs itching again, or removed breasts serving milk again, or detached hands reaching out again, I talked it over with myself.

Such events, some experts argue, are seizures, letting the brain's system run an unexpected and previously undetected course. Now I look back at my wonderful night and realize my cells worked to work, but their efforts only proved how unplugged they remain.

Don't we all have similar moments? Not always waking to stare at a fan, to enjoy rehearsing a lifetime of data in a short segment of history. Not always a surprise, a light in darkness, a noisy silence. Often, we get a glance at what might have been, what could have been, what should have been, what we wish had never been. Moments.

For charismatics, illnesses like mine cause countless problems. Apart from the naming-and-claiming doctrine that blames pain and suffering on doubt, even my mess-ups might cause mass revival. While speaking at a convention, I said, "If I pass out while speaking, I hope the not-so-spiritually-inspired have the courage to call 911 while revivalists assume I'm slain in the Spirit. My twitches and mumblings might not be an outpouring of God's power. Those seizures always keep us guessing. Medication, instead of an interpretation or revival, should follow." It got their attention. It reminded the new me to laugh.

I believe in joy and purpose. I believe in God's mercy. I also seek to improve. Now, though, I must know the new me is the me I am. To remember, I paste it in my Palm device: "Face it! Let God grace it!"

I thought it through again when I was asked to speak at a medical conference. I might have convinced myself that my writing had informed them. Maybe my leadership interested them. Maybe my speaking would inspire them. I knew better. My illness and recovery intrigued them. They glanced at my MRI results and wondered what I might say. They wanted a brain-damaged preacher to stand and speak, while they watched, listened, observed.

I chose to say yes, even though I knew. I wasn't saying yes only to them. I said it to my Sovereign Doctor who instructs me to face how my cheese has moved, to face my own disappointment with God, to face my table in the presence of enemies, to face my sinking in the water, to face the new me and still tell the old, old story.

How to do it? My damaged brain tells me that building a wall for hiding isn't the answer. Neither is waging a war of anger. Facing reality is. Viewing life through the lens of truth, letting others hold hands, feed mouths, open doors, and remind us of names. Those tasks fit the strategy for survival of the faithful. They always have.

Maybe I can learn from Jacob, refusing to let his midnight match conclude until he was blessed. If the result guarantees a lifetime limp, isn't a true touch of God worth it?

Or from David, facing a giant or a king in attack mode or a sin while still journaling poetic songs of celebration and confession. In ancient prayer closets of caves and king's courts, he released his worry to his Watcher.

Or from Paul, rejoicing while being chased by foes or jailed by religious opponents or soaked from sinking in the sea. His choice to celebrate *during* turmoil, instead of after, teaches much to a spoiled modern Christian like me.

Talking to myself helps. I try hard to remember and apply my Rs of Recovery. *Rejoice* and be glad. *React* with caution, with care. *Reach* into the lives of others even though I'm not as wise as I wish. *Receive* help from people I can trust. *Release* anger in healthy ways. *Read* and *write*. If I forget any of this, I can peek at my Palm.

My "Insufficient Memory at This Time"[15] shirt still fits. So does hope. Now, even if words flow better typing than talking, I'm not forsaken. Though shaken, I'm safe. Though limping, I'm blessed.

No, God did not warn me in advance. But with every effort to remember, God warms me with His hands. May I remember Him, the One whose name is too Holy to speak.

And I hope to share Him with a world of people whose names I can't recall.

13

This Is Your Time

D eb and I sat with a group of people as they stared at
me. The small group of writers and editors felt large;
the people made me the image to investigate, the
friend to love. They had prayed for me since the illness. What
did they think about my efforts to think, about my wrestling to
remember, about my words sounding so out of order?

Two men in the group had left God's fingerprints on my
life, marks of their Lord's love and influence. Their words,
which appear below in their entirety, explain more about the
early days of my recovery, and the "new" me, better than any
summary could.

Editor Paul Smith knew me through my writing. Doug
Beacham had served as my teacher, counselor, and mentor
when I attended college; he remains one of my closest friends
from a distance. The two worked together on a curriculum-
writing committee, which met in Orlando only months after
my sickness. God knew I needed them. These men allowed me
to speak to their group on that day I barely recall. After seeing
me, after hearing me, they prayed for me and for Debbie.

Paul and I have remained friends. He edits my writing, gives
me assignments, and encourages the doubting Chris. My first
writing assignment after my sickness came through Paul. His
view of my past helped me remember what God had done and
helped me focus on what God could do. His words, written a
year after my sickness, reveal his perspective of those days:

Last year on this date, Chris Maxwell was assaulted with a deadly virus. It left him weak, debilitated, and with memory loss.

My association with Chris began in late 1991. Doug Beacham recommended him for writing assignments. He turned out to be an excellent writer, contributing to the young adult curriculum and the devotional "God's Word for Today." Our association was editor to writer. It was basic, not very complex.

Late in 1995, Chris asked, since I was going to be in Orlando where he pastors, if I would preach for him on Wednesday night. Of course, I accepted.

Then, it happened. Chris was struck with viral encephalitis. As the date of my trip to Orlando crept up, I contacted Evangel Assembly and learned of the tragedy. I thought I would not even get to meet this brilliant writer, and that we had lost one of the best writers to the insidious virus.

However, on the day I arrived in Orlando, instead of being picked up by just Les Hall, Chris' associate pastor, Chris was in the car. He came into the hotel, and even greeted me by name (although I found out later he was coached by Les). We had a very enjoyable meal together with a great time of fellowship as we reviewed the events of the previous five weeks.

What is most amazing about Chris' illness is, in the middle of a near fatal tragedy, God began to cement a friendship that would probably not have been possible in any other circumstance. I received a burden of prayer for Chris, his wife, and kids that I have kept before God. I have received far more from Chris in his weakness than I have given him. Even in his recovery, Chris' positive, upward outlook and desire to minister to others far exceeds that of most of us.

In the months after our initial face-to-face meeting, Chris and I have kept in touch by e-mail. Although brief, the content of his e-mail has depth and insight that is nothing short of phenomenal. I have grown to love this man of God because of who he is.

Chris' wife, Debbie, has been a bulwark through Chris' entire process of healing. She has suffered as much as he has through her love for him. She has kept his appointments, done the job of both mom and dad, and held her family together while Chris was recovering (and continues to recover) from this illness. And through it all, she has demonstrated a tremendous Christian grace that could only come from someone who has been in our Father's presence.

I have noticed since Chris began writing again that both his poetry and prose have grown in quality since his brush with death. His devotionals cause readers to think beyond the words on the page. He is displaying a talent that has been tried in the fire of affliction and shown itself to be of pure gold from God.

This doesn't mean Chris doesn't make mistakes. He can be stubborn and bullheaded, and sometimes does not recognize when he needs help. But his family nudges him in the right direction, and his church is there to support him.

Chris has made wonderful progress since he collapsed a year ago. Not only in recovery, but in Christian grace and dependence on God, who continues refining the talents He gave Chris. The evidence is in his preaching and his writing. Plus his compassion for others has grown. Chris continues being a great friend and brother in spite of what is going on.

I thought about editing Paul's analysis. Writers appreciate editors rescuing them from dull drama, boring dialogue, and unnecessary adjectives, but writers also wonder why editors usually delete the writer's favorite phrases. I wanted to get back at Paul, erasing such improper wording as, "He can be stubborn and bullheaded at times." His report could display more literary splendor without that line, right? No. Paul knew my stubbornness. My family and staff said "Amen" when they read that line. As usual, an editor knew the adjectives needed to enable readers to relate. I'll not be stubborn. This time, I'll leave it alone.

I'll also ask God to help me get better at receiving His editorial services in my life. There is much more of me He needs to change.

I respect Doug Beacham as a leader and a friend. He continues to bless me as my spiritual coach. Almost one year after his friend Chris changed forever, he wrote words that remind me of my past:

I'm finally sitting down to write about the past year of your experience—truly a walk through the valley of death experience. I hope you discovered that you do not have to fear evil in the midst of such a walk. That's the promise of God—fear no evil. That allows us to fear other things and means that God may not necessarily keep us from other experiences of fear: fear of absence from the ones we love, fear of lost words, memories, dreams, fear of a lost future. But nonetheless, He is present with us in those fears.

When I first heard of your illness, I was in a personal state of shock at the sudden death of my father on Saturday, March 2, 1996. (As an aside, I've realized that one of the reasons I've delayed writing about you was a form of denial of writing about him!) When told of your serious condition, I remember thinking that I was not sure I could take this—the death of my father and of a dear friend in a matter of days. Following his death, I was caught in a burst of energy that carried me for several months. I planned, as I talked with Debbie and her parents, to fly to Orlando and visit you during those first days of hospitalization. I had the flight reserved, but Debbie told me that you were afraid (here's that Psalm again) that so many people coming to see you meant you were dying. They did not want to upset you further.

I kept in touch and remember those first phone conversations when you called me "man." I think everyone was "man" to you. I knew you knew who I was but could not make the connections to call me by name. It deeply touched me because I knew your power of words—a true gift from God—and if this were permanent, what a tremendous loss to the world!

In April, the Evangelical Curriculum Commission met in Orlando. Debbie brought you to meet briefly with us and for us to pray for you. You had written Sunday school literature for the Assemblies of God, and Paul Smith, the editor who worked with you, was there. You came and read a statement. I could tell you were nervous and still stumbling with words—yet I could tell a big difference from phone conversations just a few weeks earlier. We had prayer for you, and I remember it as one of the most moving events of my nearly seventeen years on the ECC. I also remember special prayers for your wife and children. My wife, Susan, was there with me, and her thoughts naturally went out to Debbie for all the stress she had to carry during that time, and perhaps even now. It happened to be the date of the anniversary of the Oklahoma City bombing because just before you came, the ECC stopped for the minute of silence in memory of those who died in the U.S. heartland.

Later that week, I was with you to minister on Sunday. We had supper together on Saturday night at a small Italian restaurant. You had a boldness to witness that made me ashamed of my silence. God had broken down the walls of convention that keep all of us safely hidden from one another. Your boldness was, and remains, God's way of breaking into the mundane shadows of existence of the people around you. What makes it powerful is the authenticity of your life and the anointing that comes without our awareness.

On Sunday morning, you handled yourself rather well in the service. The congregation had evident love and care for you and your family. I could tell that your emotions were still working to find the normal balance of intensity and appropriateness of intensity. This was particularly true in the prayer time before the service.

The first Sunday after Christmas, you and your family attended the Church of the Redeemer in Athens, Georgia, and you preached for us. I could tell an unbelievable difference and improvement in your speech, logical flow, and attention. In fact, I thought that our regular attendees would not think anything was wrong with you. I remember the prayer time afterward when we laid hands on several people and prayed the prayer of faith in accordance to the Word of God.

I rejoice that God has spared your life. You may, like Jacob, speak and think with a "limp," but I suspect God will use that in a special way. Don't forget, whatever the Lord is doing is more than just to and for you. It is a transformation experience which impacts your children and those around you.

As I completed this book, I wondered what perilous roads I might have turned toward or what astonishing streets I would have missed without Doug Beacham's cautions, warnings, and dares. For years, I've listened to his words. Not just regarding my encephalitis, but about life, about sinful nature and selfish desires.

While editing and rewriting my final draft of this public confession, Doug came to Orlando for a meeting. We met with friends and also took time alone. I knew the questions he would ask about my life, my family, my dreams, my desires, my inner world. He always asks. I answer with honesty. After he left, I thought about how so many people have so few friends like Doug to investigate their life's status.

While limping through the valleys and battling the war of remembering, finding what is lost and fearing an unknown future, I pray I remember the Redeemer. I pray I remember the importance of others who stare and dare. That is true care. I pray none of us shall live this life alone.

We all should find someone to call. Even if we can only call him "man."

14

How Firm a Foundation

When I briefly spoke to our congregation the first time after my illness, I tried to be me. Pausing, shaking and feeling tentative, I cried more than I ever had before from a platform. I worked to voice my words:

"Sorry, I don't understand...praying more than ever...God is teaching me...God is in control, not Chris...when I am angry God says, 'I love you'...When I say something stupid, God laughs...I do not know much, but God is real...I can't remember names, but I remember the people in those names...I love God...I remember His name...He tells me, 'Chris Maxwell, don't get discouraged.'"

I spoke. I woke a few people. They wondered: Would he change? Why did it happen? Will he ever improve? They prayed and cried as I tried to be me. Could I no longer be me? I wanted to speak and speak. Several guys came to the stage to remind me my time was up.

What did the audience think?

"We saw how much you changed," they said.

"We didn't know if you would ever get beyond that," they said.

"But we could tell you were determined," they said.

Dr. Pineless stopped me from trying too much but allowed opportunities to preach and exercise, cranking my mental engine to drive forward. He worked hard on me with wisdom and kindness.

The church's leaders needed to know more about their new pastor. They negotiated a meeting with my neurologist.

Evangel Assembly's board members wanted to hear the doctor's words themselves. They now had a pastor packed with confusion. They knew my name, but didn't know me. I hardly knew them. Dr. Pineless agreed to meet with them. At first, he wanted to make sure they were not trying to find a way to get rid of me. When my family assured him they desired the best way to deal with the situation, he arranged a gathering in his office, with two of our leaders, Debbie, and me. He answered questions, offered advice, and, thank God, believed that I should be allowed to teach. His honest assessment of my abilities balanced my personal argument with medical facts.

Jim Rovira summarized the comments so all the leaders could learn from Dr. Pineless. As always, Jim's words—which became official board minutes to protect the church's future decisions—communicated well. Along with a physical description of my condition—"Chris' viral encephalitis...caused actual physical deterioration of nerves within the brain"—Jim offered strategies for helping me. He also listed the doctor's recommendations for my recovery—"The best rehabilitation is stimulation. Preaching is very good for him in this regard." *Stimulation* is an interesting phrase Dr. Pineless used. For victims of traumatic brain injury or a variety of other life-changing experiences, therapists work hard with that word in mind. They seek methods to stimulate, motivate, inspire, prompt, and—nicely, of course—push. In other words, my health would only improve if I worked to do my part. Dr. Pineless, Dr. Attermann, Patti, and our congregation allowed me to work where I could, knowing my efforts would work to repair my mind.

Patients must not leave problems alone. To face them and let God grace them is a crucial choice. Avoiding disadvantages allows the disabled to elude mistakes and embarrassment, but it also keeps victims from moving forward.

Moving forward was what the church wanted me to do. Moving forward was what I needed to do. That is true for each of us. Do we really want to notice our strengths and build on them, while admitting our weaknesses and finding help? Moving forward, instead of moving out, works.

I asked a friend how he moved forward, learning to walk again after a car accident. He said, "I worked and refused to stop until I walked. Then every morning, I would wake up and have to force myself to walk again."

I asked a lady who had battled an eating disorder since her teen years how she moved forward. She said, "I focused on my positives and worked to improve them. I also confessed my weaknesses with total honesty and asked others to help me. If my friends had never confronted me to find help, I might not have changed."

I asked an alcoholic how he faced his addiction and won the battle. He said, "I had to admit what I was really like. For too long, I claimed not to have any problems. It helped me when I finally got help. Three times a day, I voice my vows and pleas to God in prayer. Now, four years and seven months since my last drink, I keep moving forward one step at a time."

I asked a lady if she still struggles to forgive her husband for his affair. She said, "Remember when you told me to walk through the house and read the Scriptures loudly? Things have been better since then. I know it was more than that. The counseling, the prayers, the forgiveness, and knowing he is now held accountable. But it is like something happened in the house, or maybe in my spirit, that gave me hope again. I keep hearing you say that I need to remember how God also has forgiven me. Looking back, I'm so glad I didn't just run from the situation—or murder him—like I wanted to."

I asked a friend in prison what she would say to those of us who are still living in freedom. She said, "Stop wasting time. Don't make stupid decisions. Trust me, you don't want to end up here. But I also worry about those people who keep doing things that will never get them in prison. Their habits keep them locked in a different kind of prison. I'll tell you this, I am more free here—even though I hate it—than I was living that life of drugs."

Before I ended my visit in the federal prison, I asked the young lady to pray for me. Her honesty took reverence to another level. She didn't play a game. She pleaded to a listening Rescuer. Her prayer motivated me to stop wasting time.

I remember listening to Sammy Kershaw's song "One Day Left to Live." The video and song shouted about time running out, about people running away, about those who choose to move forward and grow.

Speaking of videos, there are few that mean a lot to me. One movie I watch changes my mood. It reminds me of my own struggles to remember. I don't feel alone. Deb doesn't want to watch it anymore. It reminds her of too much. In *Regarding Henry*, Harrison Ford portrays dealing with brain damage after being shot in the head by a convenience store robber. The man he was had learned to live a life of lies, but the man he became had to learn how to live again, to live differently. The painful process made him a better man. I've watched it before completing every article I've written about my illness.

My watching and remembering continue. When *The Lord of the Rings* came out as a movie, it took me into its world. I remembered reading the novel years ago. Noticing my own wars, observing characters at battle in my mind, I stared at journey toward victory. A journey through fear and foes, partners and pain, surprises and rescues. Watching it, I felt like believing again.

The Shawshank Redemption reminds me about the routine of working toward a rescue, about how fear can hold us as prisoners but hope can set us free. *Groundhog Day* illustrates a life returning to the same day over and over again. *The Passion of the Christ* caused me to pause again, and remember.

The TV screen also worked my thoughts. *Law and Order* reinforced my training to evaluate, relate, argue, and debate before reaching a conclusion. Stories told me, and continue to tell me, so much about life. Fiction illustrates facts and notifies a mind about working again.

Since I mentioned Kershaw's song, I must confess. Music played a role in my healing. Lyrics lunge into my baffled brain;

I often remember what I can put to music. Almost any musical style finds a way to please me, but what matters most is the writing and the stream of motion. Did Vigilantes of Love know I'm the listener they offered a *Welcome to Struggleville*? I listened to David Wilcox, Bob Bennett, Mark Cohn, Pierce Pettis. Keith Green and Mark Heard sang to me here long after they left earth. John Fischer's music and his books, Phil Keaggy's guitar, Glad's voices. Billy Mann, Charlie Peacock, Carolyn Arends, Billy Joel, James Taylor, Paul Simon, Van Morrison, Delirious?, Don Potter, the new surge of praise and worship—old songs I remembered from childhood, new songs finding ways to influence my thinking. New musicians, old commercials: I could listen to all of them. And remember. Jackson Browne sang "I'm Alive" for me; he just didn't know it. Bob Bennett's song, "In the Middle of This Madness," reminded me to dance and sing and trust my Father in the middle of my own madness. I told him he wrote it just for me.

I started back reading. Slowly. Garret and Andrea Bain gave me *The Book of God* by Walter Wangerin. Keeping it close and falling in love with the flow and rhythm, I labored to read it and remember. I also started reading my other favorites . . . slowly. Eugene Peterson, Annie Dillard, Frederick Buechner, Christopher deVinck. Peterson's devotionals and Buechner's *Listening To Your Life* fit me in both size and style. Stories, creative nonfiction, poetic motion, honest confessions, practical truth. Short daily readings fit my brief attention span while still reflecting startling literature. I met Timothy Jones at a writers' conference and loved his style of writing. Kathleen Norris and Anne Lamott and Philip Yancey and Calvin Miller didn't know they wrote books to rework my mind.

I felt as if Anne Lamott challenged me personally when she wrote, "Believe in your position, or nothing will be driving your work. If you don't believe in what you are saying, there is no point in your saying it. You might as well call it a day and go bowling. However, if you do care deeply about something . . . then this belief will keep you going as you struggle to get your work done."[16]

I hit rewind and returned to C.S. Lewis's *Chronicles of Narnia*. I felt I had arrived.

I hit fast forward and read new authors. I felt a few knew me.

My eyes battled some as my vision adjusted to the new journey toward a mind seeking to interpret and remember. And I felt my intellect had become frozen and my words had been buried while my emotions pretended to be Florida summer weather, merging dangerous storms with delightful sun.

But, hey, I had started back reading. I will never stop again. Will I? And would I start back writing anything other than the desperate phrases I scribbled for survival?

Speaking of starting back, my friends remember when they didn't let me speak on a Sunday after my illness. My first Sunday sermon waited close to me. Only days away. I knew, I knew: it would differ greatly from past preaching. Before, my memory had assisted me. I rarely needed to read notes while speaking; my week of study and review readied me for Sunday teaching. This short talk could not match that, but I longed, so much, to speak.

A surprise came. Those close to me and concerned about me contacted one of my doctors. He sided with them, canceling my first sermon. Anger exploded in me. I felt subtracted, lied to, rejected. My family and friends never meant such; they had proven so much positive assistance that it resulted only from their love and concern. I should have known it.

At the time, though, I knew only that a sign of my improvement had been subtracted. I went on speaking briefly, greeting my friends in the morning services at Evangel. I felt like never before, but being up there helped me, helped me much more than even I expected. My comments exceeded the doctor-approved time limit, and leaders wanted to care for me by stopping me. So much life circled through. I cried. I thanked. I lived. I finally stopped talking.

After Dr. Pineless explained the importance of allowing me to speak, the people welcomed me back. I needed to express myself, to open up, to respond to those I loved. We need to grasp our perspective of biblical truth; that is what we need to remember. Proclaiming the truth heals us. Hearing the truth proclaimed heals us. Both speaking and receiving: each of us needs them. Yes, even a sick pastor whose sermons seemed so different as he cried, asked for help, and talked individually to members listening to him.

Even though I've never returned to being the former preacher, can't I confess my own healing and recovery? Can't we all face who we really are and begin again? Can't we grow, change and be made new? Can't we really live?

15

Seize the Day

Sitting at a table with Dr. Hal Pineless almost eight years after my illness, it was my time to ask questions. He did not hesitate to be honest.

And I thought I could eat lunch during this conversation? The chicken Caesar with tomatoes didn't taste the same.

You know doctors. They begin with questions.

Dr. Pineless asked how I felt writing the story about my struggle. He suggested I write about "how things have evolved." He wanted me to confess my new "thought process" through the journey of adjustment.

When it was my time to ask questions, I began by asking about the name epilepsy. He responded—because he is good at it, and he knew it would help me prepare for painful truth—with humor, saying, "That goes to prove what they say in the movie *My Big Fat Greek Wedding*, 'Everything the Greeks invented.'"

Since I needed to improve my low self-image, I decided to give him information. I asked if he knew that every fifteen seconds someone undergoes a brain injury. He offered a stare and a short agreement: "Oh, I believe that."

Then he took over. "You were extremely lucky that, when you came to the hospital, Lee Adler and I were both there at the same time. That rarely happens. Many things lined up for you."

"Once we knew you had encephalitis, we still didn't know what type. Encephalitis is an infection of the brain, caused by either a virus, bacteria, or fungus; it could be many things. But it's basically an infection of the brain. Herpes is the genus, the main category of viruses. There are many different types, but you had herpes simplex one. The MRI looked classic for what you would see with herpes encephalitis. So our guess proved to be correct, and we got you started on the right medicine. You had fever and seizures, so we went by our gut feelings."

Between slow bites of salad, I confessed, "God was using you guys."

Dr. Pineless agreed: "Yeah. I remember going in and seeing you whacked out. You were acting psychotic, talking nonsense. That's what a lot of people do with lesions in that area of the brain. At least you were talking, though."

I smiled, speaking words about my previous attempts to voice words: "Sometimes I wouldn't stop talking."

I thought Dr. Pineless would smile. He didn't. "In the beginning, you wouldn't. You would vary between having a hard time remembering what you wanted to say, getting frustrated when you couldn't say it, and then sometimes just talking gibberish. Over time, that started going away. When I began seeing you in the office, you felt frustration that you couldn't express what you wanted to say."

I wanted to know why it affected my emotions like that and why I would cry for no reason.

"The temporal lobe has a lot to do with emotions," he said. "The injury directly changed that portion."

Listening and eating and recording his words, I hoped to remember them. He hardly paused. "One of the things that affected you and still does is names. The area where you're damaged is the *naming center* of the brain. I remember hearing that you could remember names easily before. Now you still have to use devices and look at people you work with who can help you know a person's name. They know when Chris needs help."

Dr. Pineless needed to eat. I needed to talk. I spoke in a tone telling of my frustration: "That's never going to change, is it? I've tried every memorization trick. What worked for me before doesn't work now. Imagery doesn't work because I forget the picture I put in my mind."

His answer didn't provide a miracle. "Well, you have to find ways to adapt. That is the best you can do."

Friends came over to say hello. Both knew me before. Both knew me then. One knew me during. We all smiled and laughed. As they left, Dr. Pineless continued: "Your family struggled; we all struggled watching you. But you have a terrific family, a great wife. She went through a lot. I tried to give everybody hope. If you don't have hope, what do you have? Is it partly sunny or partly cloudy? What's the real difference? It is just how you look at it.

"You were very healthy until this freaky thing happened to you. So you had a lot going for you. You were relatively young. You didn't have other major medical problems. It was a matter of getting you through this thing. People with neurological problems and their families—and even the doctors—want to understand everything right then. It often takes two or three days for tests to reveal what is really wrong. It is a matter of being patient and sticking it out."

I asked questions and offered thoughts: "In what areas have you seen families struggle the most? Deb liked the other me much better. But some people say they like this one better."

"Well," he said, "when you go through such a life-changing experience, it has many effects. Families break up over it. The illness where I see this the most is multiple sclerosis. When a couple sees someone get MS, they try to do what they can, but then it gets so bad if the person deteriorates. It's tough. I think we say in our vows 'until death do us part,' but we're all human. Some handle it better than others."

I said, "Debbie had no clue what she was saying when she vowed in sickness and in health. She didn't know she would be like a mom to me for a while."

Dr. Pineless kept the thought going. "Well, she was. You needed her to do that. But you were always motivated. I really believe that's why you did so well. You were a fighter. I always say you are stubborn, but I mean that as a compliment. You weren't going to let it, or anybody, tear you down. In the medical system, we have to present the worst case. Doctors and lawyers don't want to give patients much hope. I just like to give people hope to live. I go to the lectures and hear it. Even when we have to say bad news, we should say it the right way. And I'm a big believer that if we don't give people hope, they won't have any point in living. So I'll be realistic and not sugarcoat things, but there is a way to do that. You found ways to do it. None of us is God. How can we give up? A doctor told my mother she had six months to live. But she lived two years to see her first grandchild. She had hope. And so did you. My mom always said, 'Where there's life, there's hope.' I think that's true. Even in your case."

Playing with words is my thing. That was my time. "Think of reversing that phrase. Where there's hope, there's life. Sometimes the reason we are still alive is that we had so much hope in us."

"That's what worked for you," he said. "It wasn't easy on you or your family. Personally, I think there are many ways you are more effective. Now people join your temple—I mean your church—because of what you've been through. You are a good listener. People want that. You can understand their difficulties instead of just quoting Scripture. The clergy need to connect with the people. You could be a great orator, and everybody would walk out of church talking about how great it was. But if they forget it, and it doesn't change them, what good is it? They need a guy who can relate one-on-one. I think you've always had it but that you can use it better now."

To turn my mood a little, to turn us from personal side to medical side, I asked Dr. Pineless to explain the type of seizures I have.

"There are basically two types. The most common types are partial complex or temporal lobe seizures. That's where your injury is, in the left temporal lobe. You might do things like staring off into space. People could be talking, and you wouldn't really be connected with the environment. Or I've had some people tell me they're aware of what's going on, but they can't communicate. Or they may do unusual things like start picking things off the wall that aren't there. That's part of the seizure. Or they could become violent, attacking others as they are coming out of the seizures. The danger is sometimes partial complex seizures can intensify to a generalized seizure. Those are the ones that can be life-threatening. It's not that often. But you heard of the Olympic athlete who had a seizure while sleeping on her stomach, then suffocated. It happens."

"Why would an illness that damaged this portion of my brain cause the electrical system of that brain to work this way?"

"Think of the brain as a bundle of electricity," he said. "The brain is your terminus for electricity in your body. A seizure, basically, is a short-circuiting of that system. So what causes that short-circuiting? Tumors, strokes, hemorrhage, scar tissue. With you, it is the scar tissue. When we look at your MRI scans, we see the scar tissue. That's where your seizure activity comes from. And you might say, 'Let's just get rid of the scar tissue.' Well, there are two reasons we don't. One, the area of the brain you have it in is in the left hemisphere, the dominant side. If we were to try to take it out—and believe me, no neurosurgeon would do this—you would have worse problems. You might not even be able to speak. The second reason we don't do it is that there is no guarantee removal would eliminate the seizures. Any time there is an instrumentation of the brain, you could create new scar tissue and more possibilities of seizures. Based on the technology we know, this isn't something that's doable."

"I've finally been able to notice when they are coming on," I told him. "But as we look to my future, will I get worse?"

His answer helped me learn about me: "You are over your worst. But at this point, you will take medicine for the rest of your life. You still need lifetime therapy. The scar is always there and can always cause a seizure. So, your problem with seizures is always going to be there. With many medicines to choose, we can maintain control for you. We need to find medicine that doesn't interfere with your ability to get along in society, so you can concentrate on what you need to do.

"Some patients fail to see they need help. Teens are often tough to control because they feel invincible. It is hard to convince them they really need help. Everybody is different.

"You needed medicine that fit you, and you had to finally face what had really happened in your life. Different patients take different medications. But I know if I ever need a PR campaign, I could get Chris to get up with his PowerPoint presentation and tell people about me."

We both laughed.

While he ate a few bites, I remembered another of his phrases: "If you don't have hope, what do you have?" Sitting in a noisy restaurant, hearing music and voices, eating a nice salad, listening to an honest friend, allowing thoughts to circle through my strange system of mental connection, I realized that I had endured my journey because of hope.

Refusing to quit allows us to stay on the field. Resisting escapism permits us to pursue recovery. Gazing through painful reality and noticing hope amid the frightening jungle inspires minds to work. Positive anticipation instigates endurance. We chase, we hunt, we race, we fall. But we stand and step forward, refusing to resign from life's journey. While eating, I remembered inner voices and outer voices echoing the dare: Do not give up. Empowered by my Heavenly Therapist, I somehow endured.

If you don't have hope, what do you have?

If you don't have it, find it. Pursue it. Refuse to quit and relinquish your role, even though you feel now as if you fit nowhere at all. Stand up for the cause. Place an order. Taste and see. Swallow and digest. Let hope remake you.

16

Up on the Roof

Are you surrounded by spies? I am. But maybe it is okay to be watched. These pages uphold the biblical theory of accountability. They declare the difference between care and control. By receiving the often picky advice of others, people can grow. It doesn't really have to be so bad to listen and learn from those nearby. As business trends promote the modern approach of team play instead of leadership demands, these scenes from my life show what corporate cooperation can bring.

How do my spies work? They ask questions. They expect honest answers. If I lie, they notice. If I change the subject, they quickly lure me back.

I remember climbing onto the roof of our house to clean the gutters. But, as often happens to writers, the world around me grabbed my attention. Little children playing. Joyful voices announcing the game. Pitching and hitting. Sliding into home.

Up on the roof, I had the perfect view.

So I wrote a story about it. Readers liked it. My neurologist didn't. He merged medical terms with normal-man phrases, warning me of the consequences of seizures taking place on a roof. He brought up subjects like gravity. He thought I would fall for his warning.

He thought he had the perfect view.

He should know. Notice his experience.

Think 15 seconds. They race as you read these words.

During that quick moment, one person in America sustained a traumatic brain injury. A much different type of "born-again experience," many of the victims will never be the humans, the husbands, the moms, the ministers, or the CEOs they were before.

Total numbers? 1.5 million Americans sustain a traumatic brain injury each year. And 80,000 of us experience onset of long-term disability following those injuries. These statistics reveal a large, confused, sad audience.

Dr. Pineless and I talked about the numbers, the facts, and my life. As he guided the dialogue again, he called himself a gourmet chef.

I continued eating, learning from the chef.

"Your medicine is good for you, but it might not be good for others. I see myself as a gourmet chef. Until 1993, treating epilepsy was forcing patients to take medicine no matter what the side effects would be. I told them to be glad we had medicine to control the seizures. Now we can fine-tune it. The biggest problem is getting the patient to play by the rules and stick with it. Too many people just want instant gratification."

To help me understand the truth of a few worries, I asked, "What about the long-term effects of my medicine? Aren't there concerns about the kidneys and liver?"

"The newest might avoid some of those problems," he said. "There are some reports coming out that it might cause lack of calcium. Usually it is the older drugs. What you're taking is one we still don't know much about. It's one drug we don't fully understand the mechanism for why it works. We think it has to do with the gabba inhibition in the brain, but we really don't know."

I interrupted. "What is that in the brain?"

"That part is one of the neurotransmitters in the brain, a place that triggers seizures. We think other portions relate more to seizures, but we aren't fully sure of why your medication is effective. It just seems to work. We are also finding other uses for it, like in treating tremors and migraines. Many are viewing seizures and migraines as closely related.

"Almost every drug affects the liver. Your medicine just about bypasses it instead of being like most of the other drugs. If it works, don't change. Some medications can affect your speech, but this seems to work okay for you.

"And you are good about taking your nap too. A lot of people are saying we all should be doing that. America would be more productive if we shut down between 1:30 and 3:30 like other nations do. Siesta times can charge everybody up, but you really need it. Many others take power naps. Don't feel bad about it."

The nap-taker asked another question. "Will I ever need more MRIs?"

"Not unless we have an academic reason for doing it. Times may change, and there may be new devices that could help you. Based on what I know now, you don't need another MRI or EEG."

And another question: "As far as my future goes, it is just me dealing with my condition, right?"

"I think it is just taking your medicine and living the life you need to live. And not worrying about it. Remember the precautions. You stay away from alcohol. You get the proper sleep. You avoid medicine that can trigger seizures. Ask the pharmacist before you take anything. Some antibiotics and anti-depression medications can mess you up."

"And I still don't have your permission to ride roller coasters?" Only one of us smiled.

With a serious expression, Dr. Pineless spoke with the tone he uses in his office. "Don't," he said. "A study has revealed that kids who were riding roller coasters five or six times started getting hemorrhages in the brain. Some developed seizures. Somebody like you, who has gone through what you have been through but is now so well controlled, must avoid it. I know you are young at heart, but they make these rides do all these different contortions; your brain is tussling all over the place. Do you really need to risk any more? What if they put you in a place where they have a flashing strobe light? In fact, many of them say, 'If you have epilepsy, don't ride this.' Nobody reads it, but they know what they are warning you about. Legally, they have it up there because it is so dangerous."

I tried to smile again, and said, "Yeah, you got on to me about that and also when I wrote the article 'Up on the Roof.'"

He was still serious. "Chris, what if you had a seizure up on the roof of your house? You need to avoid those settings. You would probably be okay, and you are usually well-controlled, but I don't want you to risk it. You might be okay on a roller coaster, but why chance it? You have a family to take care of. You've got so many people to help. Don't put yourself at such a risk just for a thrill. That's the way I see it."

"What else," I asked, "should I tell an audience of readers about my story?"

"Use your sincerity. You write about real life, and that is what readers need. Tell them what you were thinking. I'm wanting to read this as your neurologist. While you went through this, what was it like for you? It would be good to give the perspective of what you were thinking, what you were feeling, and how other people were affected by it. I'm not sure how you write that. It's your job to figure that out. I think that's what people want to hear. I've never read an account from someone who has suffered an illness like this and what they are actually feeling and going through."

He hardly paused. "Talk to your family. Don't upset the family dynamic, but hear from them. Debbie can help you. She really went through a lot. I would like to think she got stronger through it. I hope so. I would like to think everybody did. I know you did. I think maybe Debbie has discovered things in herself she didn't know about. Having her do things you used to do is not bad for her. Now you've learned to delegate and put your trust in others. When you read books about leadership by guys like John Maxwell, you can see how important it is to let others do things. So you have to do that now. That is an important thing to do. I can remember hearing from people in your church how you now rely on others better. And you know what? Stuff gets done—maybe even better—when we let go."

Moving toward the end of our lunch and our ninety minutes of confession, his voice revealed love, care, hope. "Your speech is so terrific," he said. "No speech pathologist would know what has happened to you. When people hear you speak, they can't believe this happened to you.

"You aren't just my patient. You are my friend. God has used your illness to influence my life. I've watched you and tested you. Seeing how you have handled this has helped me want to get closer to God. So, you are thanking me. But I want to thank you also."

I left amazed to hear again the medical side of my story, amazed to hear one of my rescuers thank me. I drove home in a thunderstorm, listening to upbeat music to keep me awake on the road, convincing my nap to remain on delay until I arrived back home, asking myself why that man would thank me.

The journey south took me near the hospital. I glanced east and remembered. The storm and traffic gave me much time to think and recall. It is like revisiting an ancient city, or maybe digging up the ruins to see what remains. It is like stopping long enough to stare at what is often ignored. It is like gazing at a finger, a foot, or an elbow, realizing there is so much of us we overlook. When we stop and notice, we stare in amazement.

I peeked at a doctor's office as I drove past it. I wanted to tell Dr. Steven Attermann the whole story about my lunch with Dr. Pineless. I didn't. But I remembered my recent interview with Dr. Attermann. He, too, is now my friend. He, too, has been affected by the journey he helped me endure. He never knew the former Chris.

When I meet with Dr. Attermann, we laugh. My rebellion during those first days of my illness was transported and deposited for Dr. Attermann's enjoyment. And now he rescues lives with his hair hanging down.

We've prayed together and read through Psalms. He is Jewish. I am Christian. Together, we relate about a Heavenly Father, about rescues, about my changes, about stopping to notice, about staring in amazement.

Dr. Attermann had short hair when I became sick. I had

very long hair. Now things have reversed. His hair is very long for a doctor. My hair is now cut short in the back and missing completely up top. Get my point?

My mind stopped long enough to stare into a previous conversation. I could remember a few of the words he recently said to me: "Chris, you are handling your situation great. You could have quit and given up. But you didn't. Things aren't always easy for you, but you just keep going. All I can do now is make sure you are going the right way as you keep going."

All he can do? That is a lot.

The plan for me? To keep going and going and going. Not busy-ness, but life. Not packing every moment of every day, but looking and listening, hearing and seeing.

I arrived home, still remembering. The rain hit repeat; the storm hit play.

Calvin Miller portrayed my mood on paper:

"I still understand so little, but then we are not called to understand everything about God, only to attend him. And I know that when I draw near to God, I am a prisoner of the only reality there is. The reality of the Divine Mystery."[17]

17

Graceland

I've mentioned Jim Rovira several times. Our friendship goes back to my days as a youth pastor. Now, as well as being a church leader at Evangel Assembly, Jim is a scholar, a writer, an editor, a teacher, and a friend. He wrote about my experience just a year after I entered the hospital:

Chris referred to a visit from the deacon board while he was in the hospital. I was there for that visit and remember Chris lying in his bed, looking fine, but not being fine. Being hardly able to speak coherently. Not remembering his wife's name, or his children's. I remember us praying for him. I remember him grabbing my arm as we were leaving and asking me, point-blank, "Why is this happening to me?" I said I didn't know, but that you hadn't lost a thing. I put my hand on his head and told him it was all right there. He just had to remember how to get to it again. Because, even at that stage—that early in his illness—he remembered us. Not our names, but us. Me.

I've just finished reading Chris' journal dealing with his illness. Overall, the accounts of his illness by those around him are accurate. It has now been just over a year since he first contracted encephalitis, and at times it is easy to forget he is ill, he has improved so much. In the earlier stages, when he first returned to the church, he knew you, as Mary Dement said, but not your name.

His preaching? Early on, he struggled for words, and spoke with a very low diction level. I have written a transcript of one of his first sermons in the last chapter of my senior honors thesis on James Joyce. But even in his first sermon after he was allowed back to work,

I could tell his ability to organize material had not suffered greatly. He organized much the same way he had before his illness, though not quite as well. Believe me, he was far from merely spouting out random sentences. He cried constantly, it seemed, sometimes for joy, other times from sadness. If he was angry, those around him knew it. My immediate impression was that whatever was going on inside him emotionally was exposed for all to see. I remember thinking, "It's a good thing he's a good man, because if he were otherwise, there'd be real problems."

But that problem would be that of the complete exposure of his true character. And why is that a problem? Because our true character is not something to be exposed. It is more ugly than not. Exposure is shameful because we are sinful, selfish, and childish. It is shameful for us all. Chris seems to have been selected for a purification process that is radical, but hopefully curative of the disease we all share, though seem always to have to bear alone.

This has been the basis for pastoral leadership in American churches. All that has been taken away from Chris. He cannot control his emotions. He cannot use words well. He cannot manipulate people. All he has left is God.

Jim's honest study confronts each of us. His words "looking fine but not being fine" explained me. And often, in the now, they still explain me. Until observers notice a quirk or a pause, they know little of my battle to remember. Unless informed about the purpose of my Palm device addiction or my time restrictions or my near-continual hand-washing, they might fail to notice my uniqueness. But even when I'm looking fine, I'm not really fine.

The Bible throws that toward every one of us. All have sinned, it says. All fall short, it says. No one lives just right all the time, it says.

That explains God's evaluation and broadcasts the general condition of our souls. We need help, and we can't cure ourselves. We are not what He wants us to be, and we make things worse trying to get there ourselves. The philosophies of this world fall short and do not cure what really ails us. Still, if all we have left is God, is that really so bad?

Appearances often lie. We aren't what we seem to be. Performance covers a multitude of realities. I'm not saying we should all become naked at midnight and march to the nurses' station just as we are. I'm suggesting that we get to know ourselves as we really are. And that we receive help from the Mind who already knew us, the Maker who can change us from within. He can do what we cannot. He wants us to want His help.

He comes in various ways. The Word or the wind. The sea or a song. While we pray or while we shower. When we kneel alone in prayer or when we clap with a crowd in worship. In silence or in shouts. And as I've stated, He appears in the bodies of normal people willing to represent Him to make this world a better place by displaying His grace.

So many people did just that in our lives, helping to carry the burdens that had fallen to me and my family. We had been waylaid by a disease, but these friends stopped to help us.

Mary Davis worked hard in our house, washing clothes and reading to me. I listened and cried as she read. Her care showed, some of it born in her own struggle after her husband Earl's death. I remember speaking at his funeral.

Tim and Marie Kuck continued to represent God. Tim spent time with me; Marie bought groceries and encouraged Debbie. I'll never forget their son Nathaniel's life on earth and his departure to heaven. As they cared for me, none us knew what was coming into their lives. Would I have been a better help to them during those years if my brain had not been damaged? I ask, and ask, and ask. I still miss Nathaniel and remember his name.

Ray Michaud mowed our grass, offered advice, and prayed prayers. He called, he helped, he asked, he worked. He put his beliefs into action.

So many people offering so much caring. How do lonely people face this type of emotional disease? I prayed for God to help. He helped through His Spirit and His people.

As I speak and counsel patients and their families, I hear the story often.

"Nobody understands."
"Nobody cares."
"Nobody is here to help."

I wish I could clone my caregivers and share their love. I pray other victims and their families find such care.

Now, take this personally. Though no one can fully know your inner battle, allow people an opportunity to stand beside you. Standing beside doesn't require understanding. It just takes God's love and passes it around.

My wife's parents, Stan and Eve Oliver, did that. They expressed great kindness through acts of love. My mother-in-law drove me to get food, to the office, or to see my sons. During this inning of my life, I needed her, and she stayed close to me. She lived like a mother helping me, a counselor listening, a friend caring.

She offered her tender kindness. She heard my many words. She drove me to the church that first time I greeted the people face to face, stayed there waiting for my short speech to end, and then took me back home.

When life continues after almost ending, close people can get even closer. Dialogues shift in depth and truth. Victims talk about real life.

Phone calls came. They listened to my talking. They heard my tears do much of the talking.

When my nephew John sent me my "Insufficient Memory at This Time" T-shirt, I slowly learned to live what fit me. How true! Funny, but the perfect find for his uncle. I smiled, thanking God for all His gifts. Survival. Truth. A longer life. Depending on Him, in Him. A way to find a positive scene during a negative fall. This gift of life, for which I have become more thankful than ever.

In the past—my past, so recent and familiar; my past, so distant and foreign—I could memorize. I preached sermons and taught lessons with only my Bible near. Notes could stay away.

No longer. Struggling both to read and to remember, what is a speaker to do? Is depending on PowerPoint a lack of faith? Letters from some informed me that sin, or diet, or negative confession, or lack of faith, or a generational curse, or lust, or my jokes caused the virus to attack me. My failure to use only the King James Version, one told me. My refusal to always wear a tie, one told me. My rebellious long hair, one told me. So many causes and so many results.

While they argued their self-designed doctrinal debates, I kept living, writing, and facing reality. And I cried, thanking God that our spiritual tribe did not believe that way.

I tried. Remember? Remember? Not the sermon, not the passage, not the points. I had to slow it all down. So slow. What could I know?

Passing on, time. Passing on, days. So little could I remember. So different this seemed. Could I stay calm? Could I still speak?

I slowed myself. I realized I needed to write down every key thought, not expect to remember anything. I could not spell, but usually I could tell what I wrote down.

I went to the computer to heal my misspelled words.

I went over my key thoughts. Over and over. Over and over. I still forgot. I had to keep all of it with me now.

Some of that has changed, but not completely. At that early time, I feared it would never change. I also sensed God wanted me not to worry so much about that, so I worked on my worry.

Today I am not able to remember as I could before. I work and play every trick. My brain cells feel sore. But endurance teaches lessons for the weak. Does God like it better because every verse is hard work and not just a traditional phrase easily memorized, categorized, and proclaimed? Does God want His notes to work me and work me and work me? He must. And He knows what is best.

A cruel memory reminded me of how friendly it had previously seemed. I took so much for granted. Why do we do that? We expect all positives to remain, and we want more. One slip-up and we blame our great God, asking why He didn't rescue us from our war. I have questioned Him and asked for help, but I could not tell Him He had ruined me. I knew of so many others so much worse. I hated my condition at times, but I loved God. Not understanding Him or myself, I still loved and trusted God.

I wondered often how much of my past memories would return. Names? Memorized Scripture? Events seemed to remain, and people too. My life with them I could grasp. But names? Where had they gone? Why were they hiding?

18

Rest for the Weary

eplace pure health in me, I prayed. I praised God since He saved me. People die from this disease. God kept me alive. On earth. Barely aware of all I want to know, but aware of life. This miracle! Given by God! I thank Him and ask Him for more improvement. To remind myself He does not mind me praying, I read the Word. Gospel? Good News. God's love? Amazing. I praised Him.

My firstborn son also writes, mixing melody and honesty; like what happens with many good poets and songwriters, his nonfiction life displays drama. Taylor gave his testimony to a group of youth. Friends told me what he said, and I asked for a written version of his thoughts. From his heart to mine, I received it.

Read Taylor's honesty:

When I first found out how ill my father had become, mixed anger and fear rushed through my body. I was so young. To have something like that happen to my father was cold and merciless. I began to blame God as my father struggled to return to his normal self. We knew it would take lots of time, but it was hard to respect him. It felt as if he didn't know as much as I did. And, for a while, he didn't.

I began to turn to my girlfriend for attention and replaced God as being Lord of my life with her. She had my attention, my focus, and all my time; I left God and my family in the dark. This went on for two years of an on-and-off terrible relationship until one day God broke me. I spent that day sobbing on my knees and crying out for repentance.

117

I had to leave old friends and many selfish things behind and follow Christ again. Yes, it hurt for a while, but not as much as sin was hurting me and my future. I once again was able to restore my relationship with my father and gain respect for my family once again.

Now I feel that, having God back in control and being Lord of my life, I have a freedom like never before. Now Dad and I look back and learn from what went wrong and work together to encourage our family and others. I know he is there to encourage me in my dreams and calling. Thank you, God, and thank you, Dad, for giving me a second chance.

Taylor also typed a personal addition just to me. He wrote, *"There you go, man. I hope you don't cry at all."* He knew better. He knew I would cry. A few years before, I didn't know Taylor would still love his crying father. Now it was like rest for the weary.

Rest for the weary?

The apostle Paul knew about it. Paul, another writer and friend, another leader who knew about weakness and storm and unanswered prayer. He knew about rest for the weary.

Recently, Jim Rovira and I led a Bible study together. I gave the introduction, illustrations, and practice application. I let Jim serve the meat. His mind can do things like that. The truths we studied wouldn't leave my mind, though. They stayed.

We were studying a series of the most-often quoted verses of the Bible. My plan was to clarify the context and grasp the true meaning. So instead of just memorizing and quoting Philippians 4:13, we helped the audience notice the full scene. I didn't expect to notice so much.

Paul related to hurt and disappointment. But look at his attitude from Philippians 4:10-19 (NIV):

I rejoice greatly in the Lord that at last you have renewed your concern for me. Indeed, you have been concerned, but you had no opportunity to show it. I am not saying this because I am in need, for I have learned to be content whatever the circumstances. I know what it is to be in need, and I know what it is to have plenty. I have learned the secret of being content in any and every situation, whether well fed or hungry, whether living in plenty or in want. I can do everything through him who gives me strength.

Yet it was good of you to share in my troubles. Moreover, as you Philippians know, in the early days of your acquaintance with the gospel, when I set out from Macedonia, not one church shared with me in the matter of giving and receiving, except you only; for even when I was in Thessalonica, you sent me aid again and again when I was in need. Not that I am looking for a gift, but I am looking for what may be credited to your account. I have received full payment and even more; I am amply supplied, now that I have received from Epaphroditus the gifts you sent. They are a fragrant offering, an acceptable sacrifice, pleasing to God. And my God will meet all your needs according to his glorious riches in Christ Jesus.

Paul didn't just rejoice. He rejoiced *greatly*. What was his reason for rejoicing? Had they released him from prison? Had God finally answered his prayer and healed Paul's thorn in the flesh? No. Paul rejoiced because his Philippian friends renewed their concern for him.

That makes me feel better. I'm tempted to join the rejoicing. When others encourage me and pray for me, a sense of rejoicing hits my inner world. Paul welcomed their care and rejoiced. He knew they cared for him even when they struggled to show it. Given an opportunity, they showed their concerns.

Notice his next confession. He assured them he wasn't sneaking in a plea for more care and concern. In fact, he broadcast total honesty about how he had learned to live this hard life of reality.

When Jim and I taught this, we emphasized the often misused verse, Philippians 4:13. I've quoted it in so many ways that just never worked. I quoted "I can do all things through Christ who strengthens me" when I played high school basketball. But I never dunked the ball. Instead of using it as a lucky charm, Paul placed it in his note as a confession of reality. In what context could he do all things? In every way the Higher Power handed the prison dweller the strength to do it.

And look how God handed Paul that strength. God taught Paul to be content in every situation. That is a rare accomplishment. Whatever the circumstances, this leader of the early church did not say he escaped prison by God's power; instead he wrote, "I've learned to be content."

Read the word again: *content*. Read this one: *contentment*.

Think of your prison, your bondage, your thorns in the flesh, your unanswered prayers, your feelings of rejection, your poor vision, your unfulfilled dreams, your damaged brain, your chemotherapy, your medical expenses, your never-ending pain. Think. And ask: Am I content?

I think of my thinking. It feels like bondage, like prison. I think of my thinking and ask myself: Am I content? Right here, right now—am I content?

Paul took his thoughts further. He knew about being in need, and he also knew about having plenty. He knew contentment when having leftovers to put in the freezer and also when not having enough fresh milk for his Honey Nut Cheerios or a modem for his computer. More importantly, he knew *contentment* when living in either condition, in plenty or in want. And he emphasized the positive by confessing how he endured such extremes of life: "I can do everything through him who gives me strength."

Then, he went another step, writing: "Yet it was good of you to share in my troubles." Even though Paul had endured and survived, even though he learned the life of contentment, even though he often lived distant from those in whom he had invested so much of his life, he felt they had entered his world of trouble. From a distance, they related. In much different settings, they cared. Fulfilling roles unlike Paul's, they honored him by joining in his pain.

They gave more than others, and their aid marched into his heart. Their care invaded his world. Isn't that healing? Isn't that love? Isn't that remembering those who forget?

The gifts given, Paul said, not only pleased him. They pleased God.

How could he add another sentence after that? I mean, we can almost smell the aroma he describes. We can almost hear his grateful voice and notice his gentle tears. But his next sentence of prayer reminds us of reality: "And my God will meet all your needs according to his glorious riches in Christ Jesus."

"You did all this for me," Paul said. "Back at you," Paul said. "But not from me. From God, the Giver of All. From Him, every need you have will be met."

Do you hear what I hear? Do you hear Paul the prisoner voicing a promise to you?

"Every need. Met. By God, every need met."

Read those words. Pray those words. Receive and believe those words.

And when you are weary, rest.

19

Every Breath You Take

"The human brain is the most complex of organs—an intricate network of some 200 billion nerve cells and a trillion supporting cells. The brain controls all bodily activity, from heart rate and movement to emotion and learning."[18]

While my nerve cells and supporting cells work to figure it all out, I want to do my part to guide my brain. Every thought counts. Too often, when we feel none of our efforts count, we turn our smiles into sadness. Hurt becomes anger. Are we then better? Or have bitter thoughts and feelings packed our baggage with dangerous ingredients?

Confess bitterness. It is good for the soul. Then convert it. Not with a fake smile, nor with a tongue-lashing that gives momentary pleasure but long-term hurt. Instead, smile, grin, chuckle. Imagine a comedy show. A picture, a story, a scene.

One of my favorite such moments was when I met Larry after a funeral where I spoke. A friend introduced us, a friend who knew we had things in common. We talked about ourselves. Both knowing brain damage, both feeling like our weaknesses tended to defeat our strengths, we had only known each other a short time but felt like friends from a previous life. We might have been friends before; neither of us could recall. Instead of getting stuck there, we moved on. He told a story, wanting me to laugh. We took turns, telling and laughing and allowing humor to calm our inner storms. We thanked our

Maker for keeping us alive and for helping us face the battles of brain damage.

I remember another example, a time when God's grace made bitter water sweet. After one of our home group meetings, Terri Franklin could tell I did not like to fall short. That Sunday night, as I did many nights—the later in the day, the worse my brain performs—I had forgotten too many words. She saw I felt disturbed. Yes, I was better, but my continuing failure to return to a completely normal brain bothered me. She wrote a note to encourage me.

Dear Chris,

It's my turn to write you a letter!

I know that you are having a hard time, not being able to spell or read some words. I could see it in your face at home group. If you were struck dumb, me and everyone else in that room last night would love you (and learn sign language for you). More than us, Jesus loves you! He is using you more now than ever.

I don't know how long you will have to go through this or if it will end, but I do know that you are going to be ok. I have never felt smart or good at anything, but there has always been the one stubborn friend who always made me feel special. I bet you can't guess who he is. You have always been there for me to encourage me. So I will return the favor until Jesus comes back.

Love,

Terri

Keep that chin up, Mr. Maxwell!!

She shared from her heart, and her honesty meant so much to me. My friends cared. Many people love preachers as long as the minister does exactly what they want the way they prefer, but true believers stay true lovers. The right way for the right reasons, with no end. As most pastors do, I longed for a bigger congregation. It broke my heart when people would leave. God had blessed me, though, with a group of people who knew true commitment. And they lived it.

But I wish my forgetfulness came in sequence. It doesn't. I can't control my lack of memory or my weaknesses or my thoughts. I can work to make them work; I can organize

myself to prepare for what I expect; I can seek to usher my
thoughts using proper tips. Still, people battling MTBIs
face memory problems that include much more than "simple
forgetfulness. They can involve the inability to recall events or
to digest new information and ideas. The way you remember
is also influenced by factors such as attention, organization,
motivation, and fatigue, any or all of which may be affected by
brain injury."[19]

What shall I do then? I seek to make every day of value. I
realize I need help from God and His people. I also know that I
still know so little. Life teaches me truth as I grow old.

Debbie never liked my long hair. One nurse tells me she still
remembers my "nice, full head of blond hair" while watching me
lose my mind. I don't think there is a connection between those
two facts, but I guess we'll never know. Some church people
think I should not have had long hair as a preacher. It was
more important than their drinking or smoking or cussing or
gossiping. A few people actually liked our church better because
I was the preacher with the long hair. But Debbie never liked it.

After counseling a couple in my office, I drove home
hearing a Voice. I don't think Deb shipped her voice through
the sound waves, but who knows? I actually felt convicted
after explaining to a couple about true love, about dying to self,
about 1 Corinthians 13.

While I was driving home, God made it simple: "Cut
your hair." So I surprised my wife and sons. Since my seizure
medicine would help me become bald a little earlier than my
genes demanded, why not balance the shrinking head of hair in
advance? It worked for her. I still miss my hippy self.

I also still hope to realize that every day, every breath, and
every decision are important. While laughing, we can live with
honor. While smiling, we can cry real tears. While losing in our
selfish game, we can win the games that really matter. When
brain cells delay and when blond hairs are cut away, we might
see life a little better than before. If we choose to.

What, though, is life's finish line? Can a few words and
scenes show us more about it? Although my life changed, I'm

living here. I believe that fact won't last forever. One day I'll die. I observe it so often in the ministry. Funerals, final beats of hearts, questions about eternal life. What can we, the healthy and the ill, learn about our lodging in Forever Land? And what can we do to make each day here a success?

In my friend's hospital room, the silence sounded noisy. Two nurses. A pastor. A patient. It was just the four of us. Three watching and caring, and one lying in bed—connected to machines, wearing few clothes, taking breaths in an atypical rhythm, and waiting to leave.

How much did he know? Did he wish family members were there watching and waiting? At least one of them? How long had it been since he saw them?

We all nodded, noticing the time. They disconnected the patient's plug to life. We returned to watching and waiting. The three of us stared at the one on a stage of sickness, of sadness. Or maybe on the stage of makeover, of renovation.

Then it stopped. All of it. A heart stopped beating. Lungs stopped breathing. A friend stopped living in that place, at that moment. Our hearts, as they continued beating, felt he had entered a better place. The body wasn't up for any more days, but the spirit was. Departing from us brought this elderly friend a freedom from bondage.

The nurses left. I stayed and stared. Then I noticed his charts. I stopped, shocked, gazing at a date.

The date of his death was the date of his birth.

***

Think of you. Think of now. If today was your day to be disconnected from machines, who would be there holding those hands soon to turn cold? Whom would the doctors call? What would you want said about you after you left earth?

I remember standing beside another lady as we watched her husband's final breaths. They started attending our church after my illness, so they only knew this me, but I was fine for them. Their kindness felt good. Her nursing skills gave her an expert vantage point and a painful awareness of her husband's journey toward death.

Dr. Attermann and I looked at his dying body and spoke to his departing spirit. He was ready for a new venture, a journey toward mystery and majesty. His wife, a few family members, two nurses, two doctors, and his pastor watched and waited. For a short time, we left his wife there alone. When she felt ready, she invited us back in.

We talked to her husband and prayed to their God. We released a spirit from a defeated body. We all noticed a victory then, there. Tears came, but calmness ruled. Again I stared. I thought. I hugged three necks and walked away.

Instead of going to the waiting room, I toured the hospital and thought back. I walked to the room I remember from my near-death experience. The room was empty. I walked in. I stared out a window that appeared stranger to me then.

Glancing at my chest, I noticed each breath in my lungs, felt each beat of my heart. The machines were off; nothing was attached to my arms. My mind snatched all it could gather, and I left the room.

Breathing, I left and looked for ways to help.

Breathing, I remembered to give credit to the Miracle Worker.

Breathing, I hugged my friend and heard her say this about her husband: "He won't be here in this hospital anymore." We walked into a room and talked some more.

Breathing, we prayed again.

20

Great Is Thy Faithfulness

Having asked God if I should leave the church and no longer serve as pastor, I sensed a call to remain. I had hoped to be there a long time, but my weaknesses unearthed feelings of almost wanting to leave. To rescue that church, in some of my thinking, I needed to step aside. But the leadership team and I determined I should remain.

During one week, our church said hello to a newborn child, then said goodbye to a believer who left the earth. During one week, we learned about love, while the next one taught us about wrath.

I had pastored for ten years before my illness. I had prayed daily for twenty years and longed to see so much more accomplished. But connected to the hopes and dreams, wedded to their extremes, I found a deep thankfulness. A different type of gratefulness than I knew before. It was one I needed, and it was good.

In some ways, my life has improved. In many ways, I feel weaker and weaker, but I still love people. Disappointments do bother me, and setbacks bring frustration. I am learning to lean on everlasting arms to amble over obstacles.

Mary DeMent wrote a more recent assessment of my changes:

To me, Chris is more than fine considering what he has been through. I tell my friends that they would not notice any difference. And it's true. Those who don't have regular contact with

Chris would probably not detect any changes in his behavior, his sermon delivery, etc.

Sometimes, though, I notice subtle changes. For instance, Sunday. He struggled reading a certain word during his sermon. The word was posted on an overhead PowerPoint presentation. Something he never used. He held sermon notes. Something he never did. He wiped his mouth repeatedly. Like a nervous habit. Something he never had.

He struggles to remember names, not faces. Addresses, not places. Most middle-aged people can relate. But not Chris. He never, ever, struggled in that way. He would deliver his entire sermon, including lengthy portions of Scripture, note-free.

I often wonder the toll his memory loss has had on him. When someone we know dies, we grieve. We cry, doubt, bargain, and later accept. Surely, he must grieve the loss of the skills he once possessed.

I wonder what stage of grief he is going through, or does he go in and out? It must be difficult. Sometimes he talks about it; most times, from my vantage point, he keeps the pain to himself.

My illness has allowed God to provide opportunities for me to talk about Him. I was invited to tell the story of God's healing to young baseball players at a camp hosted by pro players and coaches; I was encouraged to challenge listeners to make sure they lived ready to face the end of life. At a nursing school, I was asked to teach about my Pentecostal beliefs, and the questions confirmed an eagerness in the people. To strangers and friends, publicly and privately, officially and unofficially, words rolled from my past frustration and into lives filled with questions.

I long for people to know their Creator loves them. Sounds so simple, seems so certain—but life proves otherwise. Too many doubt that the One who knows it all can care that much.

As time travels, I hope to move on too. Spiritually, not geographically. *Closer to the Great King*—those five words clarify it. I committed to read the Bible through during the year, a practice I once did every year before focusing primarily on individual passages over long periods. I began taking prayer walks, calling on the Boss to move, not only upon me, but upon a city that people around the world rush to visit. I write and preach my confessions. Personal stories and parables shout to an audience of honest dreamers.

I organize to realize reality. I strategize to memorize information. The tricks of this trade of working the mind include repetition and rhythm, images and extremes. I turn assignments into songs; I write myself notes while driving on dangerous roads. Will my work to recall cause a crash, or will I learn to balance caution and common sense? Memory techniques become games as my giants and my metaphors mix and mingle. I would cross an "i" and dot a "t" if my computer napped. I pause in the middle of a conversation and can't return to my flow. But I'm alive and learning.

As time travels, I hope to continue loving the people I have loved. God has blessed me by placing me in a family of people. I have friends, Christians and non-Christians. I want to stay close and become a better friend.

As time travels, I hope to remember the ride I am on, to live every day realizing how close I am to death. And contemplating life after that. A skeptic? No, a realist, but one who is full of hope and help, driven with a consciousness of victory. I have always loved to win, so why not spend forever in victory?

Mountains wait. Turns test us, asking which way we should go. Traffic slows, and we slam on brakes. Friends leave, lovers fight. Trees fall, floods tarry. Our reactions aren't up to God. They're up to us. He will do what He can do; that's what He does. He does what we cannot do. But He waits. He waits. For a cry, for a request, for a shout, for obedience.

In sickness or in health, how do we view Him, respond to Him?

Better or worse, richer or poorer, how do we know Him, live with Him?

Alive and learning.

Mattering the most in life? Issues that might mean little or much, depending on the moments. Spiritual reality, though, stands taller than all else. We forget or neglect. When reminded, we turn for a brief period. The call of God, though, the call of God continues and comes to us. Hear that? Do we hear that? That fact, heard by faith, not by feelings. That fact, that my Creator loves me and gives me life through His Son's death. He fills me with His Spirit. Though shocked or amazed, *amen,* let it be so. I say to myself, *Let it be so.* I preach and write and whisper and shout to others: *Let it be so!*

John and Judy Padgett illustrate how our congregation adjusted and decided to love both this Chris and the other Chris. On the eighth anniversary of my brain damage, Judy sent me her thoughts:

It's hard to believe that your illness was eight years ago. You truly are a miracle! I know the hindrances you live with make life challenging, but I think about all that you can do considering what could have been. God does have his reason and purpose. Even I wish I knew or could figure it all out.

I'm reminded sometimes how we first met on a Wednesday night so long ago when I showed you around the building and the tough phone calls when you were helping us through the pain our church was facing. I can't believe that was 14 years ago. So much has changed since then, and so much has happened. I pray that I have changed over time and grown. Still, God continues to shape my character and work on me to improve.

We have been through a lot together. I thank God that our friendship has lasted above changing church positions, decisions that didn't make sense to me, and the little things that I may not always agree with. Life is constantly moving and moving us around. We can't stand still in any one place. We must change with it or become bitter and cold.

Thinking of your illness brings back memories. Even the Bible says, "And it came to pass." I'm glad the event of 8 years ago has passed for you even though you deal with present difficulties. Thank you for seeing me and many others through all of our spiritual illnesses over the years. . . .

Your long time friend, Judy

Once upon a time, so much changed. This life I loved and lived changed so quickly. I could hardly adjust, could hardly understand when time traveled so suddenly and seemed so strange. Days and nights of deep despair visited regularly.

I now remember only parts of those days and nights. I still cannot remember every name, number, or word, but I can recall a life-changing experience. I have to remember it. Time, as always, has traveled to a new spot. Now, thank God, my life has lifted to a new start.

Certain reminders remain with me today. I hope they stay tomorrow. Think about them. Notice how simple calls can become wonderful gifts. Smile at the small blessings. Understand a human's inability to do it all. View life from a big perspective. Love one another. Remain humble at all times.

I know more but I wonder: Will I pray as fervently in the next six months as I did in the first, sick six months?

Once upon *this* time, is Father getting through to you? Within each moment, the Spirit can guide us. Through us and to us He can work His miracles. His calls can keep us waiting, ready. His calls remind us of the greater issues of life.

Place Peter's words inside the uncertainty of pain, sent to those whose faith was attacked: *"Dear friends, do not be surprised at the painful trial you are suffering, as though something strange were happening to you. But rejoice that you may be overjoyed when His glory is revealed."* (1 Peter 4:12,13, NIV)

Consider how Jesus described hardship: *"Blessed are those who mourn, for they will be comforted."* (Matthew 5:4, NIV)

David sang through his joy and sadness: *"The Lord is my light and my salvation—whom shall I fear?"* (Psalm 27:1, NIV)

We need these peaceful perspectives during our hardships. Looking back, I see more than I could see during my struggle, yet every day will bring new joy and new uncertainty. Through it all, we will one day and some way be comforted through Him.

Upon one moment of time, surrender all. Upon all time, serve Him. And do not forget that *that* time is *this* time. Surrender now to God and serve Him upon all time.

Suffering can, if we let it, make us better instead of worse.[20]

Conclusion: The Great Adventure

Feeling good in my Sunday morning mood, I stood with the congregation as we sang. My hopes high and my family nearby, I longed for God to guide our time together.

Then, while singing a song of worship, my mind began to wander, to wonder. Instead of voicing the words, I decided to think about them, to analyze them, to compare my praise to my personal world.

Had God really turned my mourning into dancing? Am I actually unable to stay silent? As voices proclaimed those musical phrases, did I keep with the rhythm of truth I applied or hopes I hold? My brief critique revealed facts about me.

I meant what I was singing. Like never before, I really meant it.

Why "like never before"? The B.C. (before crisis) Chris didn't know as much about complete dependence on God. The A.D. (after disease) Chris knows little else. Finally, now that I face daily mental and emotional battles, now that I can relate to valleys of the shadow of death, now that I can grasp limps and therapy and desperation and medication, I am able to mean the songs I sing. Since suffering through encephalitis, the new me knows about sickness and sadness. The new me also knows true gladness. My disability gives me a new ability to know God. Old theology plus new reliance equals true faith. Honesty plus confession guides a disappointed heart in that joyful journey: from Mourning Road to Dancing Boulevard.

My weakness equals God's strength? Yes. Thanks, Paul, for the quote.

Joyful nourishment waiting and prepared, placed on a table near my enemies? Yes. Thanks, David, for the song.

What about you? What about your mourning, your groaning, your secrets locked in the caves of private pain? Maybe these thoughts have helped you sing in tune with God's true hope.

All of us struggle. Too many of us fear admitting the truth about our weaknesses. Parents watch children die, run away, or become addicts. Pastors hear votes demanding their departure. Worship leaders lose their voices. Ministers' spouses question every Sunday if the reverend on stage will practice his preaching at home. Doubt, abuse, anger, lust, cancer, pornography—the list of pitfalls is long. Healthy spiritual hearts remain possible, though, even when veins are blocked and tests become the norm.

My damaged brain tells me that building a wall for hiding isn't the answer. Neither is waging a war of anger. When we face reality, though, viewing life through the lens of Truth, we implement the best strategy for survival of the faithful.

Leonard Sweet wrote, "Crisis doesn't make a person. It reveals you for what you are. You don't know who someone is until adversity comes. It shows the cracks, and the cracks are where God leaks through."[22]

This book has attempted to let God leak through.

Calvin Miller confessed, "A healthy child is somehow very much like God. A hurting child, his son."[23]

This book has chosen to speak of health and hurting, of God and feeling like a child.

I've pasted Dallas Willard's words in my Palm device: "I have found God's address. It is at the end of my rope."

***

I pray these pages have helped you deal with your end-of-the-rope moments; they have helped me. I pray we have all learned more about finding God's address. I also hope we never stop learning about how God really guides us, even when the roads are rocky and the curves bring fear. On this planet, we all get dizzy at times.

But isn't it an adventure? Can't it be great to live and learn, to love and laugh, to cry and survive? And can't each of us notice what we normally ignore?

I think so.

Dave Dravecky, former pro baseball pitcher and cancer survivor, words it this way: "Without a functioning deltoid muscle, I had lost certain kinds of motion. The purpose of therapy was to retrain my shoulder to use other muscles. But there was no guarantee that the full range of motion would return. A lot of it depended on my motivation."[24]

Let us support suffering leaders. Let us serve them. That service, that caring, during both our sick days and our healthy moments, can truly make us better. And let us give God time to turn each of our own battles into seasons of celebration. As we limp, let us dance. It will, in internal and eternal ways, make each of us better.

In the middle of our madness, or sadness, let us dance.

A Fellow Traveler's Guide to
Changing Your Mind

Chapter 1

* Listen - A Story:

This part of the book tells stories about painful life-changing experiences. It shows how disappointment can lure people closer to God and others. Before you go further with my story and before you read short narratives about people finding victory in painful seasons, think about you. Listen to your own story. Begin writing your testimony. And yes, the first four letters of that word spell "test." No grading. Just honest confession. Release your true tale to your Kind Counselor. Write it. Read it. Pray about it. You will be glad you did.

* Learn - A Strategy:

Write about you, just as you are. Make plans about ways to fall in love with life again.

* Lend - A Statement:

Deuteronomy 31:23 (NIV)

"The Lord gave this command to Joshua son of Nun: 'Be strong and courageous, for you will bring the Israelites into the land I promised them on oath, and I myself will be with you.'"

* Look - A Smile:

As you read your story, think of a friend or foe who might have a similar history. Go out of your way to get politely in their way. Be their missionary student, their Ed, their rabbit. Encourage them with a moment of kindness.

* Let Go - A Surrender:

moments of a new mentality,
as mysteries make an impression
over all of this, yes, all of this

in me now and on me now.
God
knows what has been done and
God
knows what to do and
God
knows how to do it all;
standing tall, seeing me and knowing me,
standing tall, a Father forming a future
for His child; that is my
God.

Chapter 2

* Listen - A Story:

Jackie Curls, the nurse who knew me, the nurse who assured the doctors, "Chris isn't like that," has also faced many challenges. She and her husband, Shep, have two sons, Preston and Nolan.

Preston is an amazing young man battling cerebral palsy. I have always been in love with Preston. Though his words are hard to understand, I feel as if he understands so much more about life than the rest of us. Jackie dealt with Preston's health and then suffered herself after Nolan's birth. Even in their rough moments, Jackie and her family always displayed true care for me and many others.

Where is a Preston or a Jackie near you? Instead of avoiding, invite. Instead of ignoring, show interest. When I visited the Curls' house recently, I had hoped to encourage them. But as Preston served me homemade ice cream and as we fished and played ball, he was the leader. I was the learner.

* Learn - A Strategy:

Write about you and how your inner life can be saved again. Make plans about ways to fall in love with life.

* Lend - A Statement:

James 1:2-4 (NIV)

"Consider it pure joy, my brothers, whenever you face trials of many kinds, because you know that the testing of your faith develops perseverance. Perseverance must finish its work so that you may be mature and complete, not lacking anything."

James 1:2-4 (*The Message*)
"Consider it a sheer gift, friends, when tests and challenges come at you from all sides. You know that under pressure, your faith-life is forced into the open and shows its true colors. So don't try to get out of anything prematurely. Let it do its work so you become mature and well-developed, not deficient in any way."

* Look - A Smile:
Notice a person with many questions about faith. Instead of rushing them toward theological correctness, begin with a smile. Let them know you care. One nurse who smiled at me gave me hope.

* Let Go - A Surrender:
(portions from the journal they found near my hospital bed)
Monday:
Wanting in the hostpitall, preparing for when we are heal and readed. The place is the Florida rosspital, by questioness enalimed me but I could find noting. Finally, I am slorry getting better. Debbe comes to me everyday, I see the bouys for a while each day Taylor, Aaron and Graham. I forgen this neames, but I love their presence and the fon we enjoy together. I pray that God will hely me get offer this group...as we triy to remember. God's pwer is the anwers. This proplem has left me week: I have know littphe, to unsher, but conetinue thowing my self beack aguide the openees.

God lokes us. He wants to to owe him, to love others and neath another to other. This weke have mad it difficulties. The expert workers ans we if know the darts, but I easity forget the people that love me. I'm trried to be faithful with him because God is ansere and peope are watchd

Tuesday:
I am tired today. I am praying for God to help me, to set me free, to heal me compleatly. God is loving, God is true, but I need to understand what is going. For instance: Why did this happen to me? How did this happen? Why did this haypen? I am heady to heatern.

Chapter 3

* Listen - A Story:

Virgil Pittman, Wycliffe Bible Translators' chaplain, pastored and served in missions for many years. He and his wife, Diane, relate to suffering in times of leadership. After fulfilling the call to become missionaries, God did not inform them in advance He would return them to the States. Virgil says, "One word captures our feelings: failure! We worked hard to become missionaries and thought we would stay."

While they served in Bolivia, South America, Diane injured her back. Their stove blew up, throwing her across the kitchen. "Dealing with leaving Bolivia wasn't easy," Virgil says. "Still, when someone asks about Bolivia, it only takes a moment to be back there emotionally."

Diane and Virgil, though they didn't know me before my illness, pray for me. We can pray for each other with a new grasp, aware of pain's permanent dwelling on earth. Virgil admits, "At times I wanted to blame someone. Much of my recovery came because a missions administrator kept in contact, assuring me of his love and prayers. Ministers in deep trial should seek someone to pour out their hearts with."

* Learn - A Strategy:

Write about you, and how the lights have gone *down* in your inner city. Plan ways to fall in love with life again.

* Lend - A Statement:
Psalm 10:1 (NIV)
"Why, O Lord, do you stand far off?
Why do you hide yourself in times of trouble?"

* Look - A Smile:

You don't need to dress like a nurse or a doctor. No license or degree needed. Just be there to give a look of hope to someone as they return to their room, their world, their life of sadness. Pray they also smile in their dreams.

* Let Go - A Surrender:

(portions of the journal they found near my hospital bed)

Wednesday:

I am ready to get home. God, please hell me, help me, get over me! Why all of this? I do not know, but I am ready to get it all over. I pray that the propblem will end quickly, that God will over come me. I am ready for the trouble to end, for the freedom to return. Deb & the boys are just what I need, and all my people are some to be here some. Why did this happen? How can all this happen to me? I am ready and praying for God to work a myracle. Please, God, do the work! I don't know why it happened. I don't know why I deserved this. Why it turned this way I do not know. Now I am praying for God to work a myracle. I need God to work. I am hoping for a myracle. Please God. I don't know why this happened.

Chapter 4

* Listen - A Story:

During my mother's ~~worst~~ times of battling cancer, I saw so much life in her. I would drive her to Atlanta for chemotherapy. When our two-hour journey north brought us back home, she found ways to gain enough energy to visit elderly friends and encourage them. The sick one brought healing. The one dying brought real life. I wonder how each of us can be more like that?

* Learn - A Strategy:

Give somebody a ride. Take them where they never thought they could go on their own. Hear the heavenly voice say, "I am with you."

* Lend - A Statement:

Psalm 35:22-23 (NIV)

"O Lord, you have seen this; be not silent.
Do not be far from me, O Lord.
Awake, and rise to my defense!
Contend for me, my God and Lord."

* Look - A Smile:
Glance at a person you have known for many years. Talk about good times. Walk together and remember. Do not let the past be lost in the rush of today.

* Let Go - A Surrender:
Time goes on I guess. Hospital workers do their thing for me and to me. Am I awake or asleep? If this is a dream it is a nightmare. Night after night. Day after day.

Speed changes here. My thoughts change here. My memory cannot control me, cannot keep me sure like before. In some ways I feel so confident but later I will find how mixed up I am. Many people are worse than I am. Many.

Does that help me though?

Chapter 5

* Listen - A Story:
Jim Hukill's voice draws a crowd. His singing, his preaching, his humor: powerful truth. As he sits in his wheelchair, he testifies about hope through disabilities, strength in weaknesses. His ministry, Eleos: The Care Network, Inc., motivates the hurting. Though battling muscular dystrophy, he rolls past one barrier after another.

Listen to him sing and speak. Read his words. Learn about life from his chair. His perspective might give you a brand new ride.

* Learn - A Strategy:
Write about your family, and how people in your local church have been welcomed by you. Plan ways to display true love to people, even to those you might not like.

* Lend - A Statement:
Psalm 28:7 (NIV)
"The Lord is my strength and my shield;
my heart trusts in him, and I am helped.
My heart leaps for joy
and I will give thanks to him in song."

* Look - A Smile:
Instead of ignoring the person in a wheelchair, give him or
her a new gaze. You don't have to stare. Just smile. Speak to
them and invite yourself into their world. They don't want to
be ignored. And many of them can teach others how to really
smile.

* Let Go - A Surrender:
*Though back home, though better, some days seem so bad. I get angry
more quickly. I also get hurt in ways like never before. Be still, be still, be
still. Know, know, know. He is God. I need to know, to accept, to take it
in, to be taken over by Him. I need Him. He wants me.*

Chapter 6
* Listen - A Story:
It wasn't easy for Les and Dianne when they led a
congregation through my illness. It wasn't easy for them a few
years later when God instructed them to step out and become
missionaries. Obedience sounds good, doesn't it? Our "in God
we trust" theology is often a painful test when He invites us
into unfamiliar territory. They obeyed. I know God can use
them to encourage people globally. They showed His love into
our lives.

Contact Les and Dianne to offer your prayers and support:
halll@ywamsfi.org

Youth With A Mission - Strategic Frontiers
P.O. Box 60579
Colorado Springs, CO 80960
719-527-9594

* Learn - A Strategy:
Ask yourself how you are really doing with your trust in God.
Give His love a chance to really break through.

* Lend - A Statement:
Isaiah 63:9 (NIV)
"In all their distress he too was distressed,
and the angel of his presence saved them.
In his love and mercy he redeemed them;
he lifted them up and carried them
all the days of old."

* Look - A Smile:
List the Top Ten Things you want said about your stay in a
hospital. Add a little humor.

* Let Go - A Surrender:
*"Ease my troubles that's what you do." Van Morrison sings it. I
confess it to my Master. Ease them, God. Ease them, God. I listened to
the song. Morrison's voice, to me, offers the hope just as he should. I tried
to join with him, singing a prayerful hope unto a listening God.*
Did You listen, God? That's what You do.

Chapter 7

* Listen - A Story:
Do you realize some of the people in your church community
struggle with major weaknesses?

Temptations attack them. Some people are haunted by past
mistakes and failures. Others are tormented not by what they
have done, but by what they are simply capable of doing. A
friend of mine, Chad,* has admitted to me that he struggles
with homosexual lust. This man is a born-again Christian
and has never actually had sex with a man. But he lives with
constant guilt about his perverted inclinations.

"I know God loves me, Chris," my friend says. "But the pain
is sometimes unbearable when I allow my mind to wander. I
can't even get near a men's fitness magazine without feeling

146

the magnetic attraction. Sometimes I even entertain sexual fantasies about my friends. It is a painful burden, but when I feel it is crushing me, I call out to the Lord for fresh grace."

I constantly remind Chad that he is not alone—and that every Christian must learn to walk above the temptations of the flesh. But Chad often falls into the trap of thinking that his sin is worse than everyone else's. "Let's be honest," he says. "To most Christians, homosexuality is the sin we don't forgive. It's in a category by itself. And I feel like I am stuck in that category." * Not his real name.

* Learn - A Strategy:
Ask, "What can I do for others that no one will notice?" Ask, "How can I voice or display my acceptance of someone whose lifestyle is against my beliefs?" Ask, "How can I warn them of their wrong while not getting in the way of their change?"

* Lend - A Statement:
Psalm 69:1 (NIV)
"Save me, O God,
for the waters have come up to my neck."

* Look - A Smile:
Make an unexpected call or send a surprising note to a friend. Think of a person who endured difficulty with you. Decide to thank them for it. Today might be the day they need your smile.

* Let Go - A Surrender:
Tears would leak quickly. Temper rose rapidly. Small, common issues grew to become giants.

I prayed, I cried, I wanted, I waited. For release. For healing. For help. Help, certainly covered me completely, but the flesh longed for more; I longed for more.

People. God sends people.

Chapter 8

* Listen - A Story:

As I interviewed Patti, I watched her feeding her mother. Slowly, Patti's Mom took bites of food. Slowly. I talked some to Patti's mother, but her words made little sense. But she always seemed to smile.

Patti's kindness now served her mother. At home, she took care of the one who raised her, an interesting reversal of roles. It is common these days, especially with the many patients like Patti's mother battling Alzheimer's. While I write about my brain change, I can still read the latest statistics. What do they tell us?

That in America 4.5 million people suffer from Alzheimer's disease. As I write this and as you read it, one out of three of us knows someone battling it. People live an average of eight years, or maybe as long as 20 years after the initial diagnosis. The average cost of care is $174,000. (info from http://www.alz. org/AboutAD/statistics.asp.)

But even as we notice numbers and chart statistics, let us remember the people. One life, one mind, one heart at a time. One story can, if we allow it, help our life stories become better.

* Learn - A Strategy:

Read about Alzheimer's. Visit a friend who struggles with it or one who has a family member facing it. Make a list of what you learn about life as you watch their new world. How can you become better? How can you help those who care for them?

Remember Patti's words: "Let's call it motivated; you were definitely not going to be stopped." Be motivated and refuse to be stopped as you help others.

* Lend - A Statement:
Psalm 23:4 (NIV)
"Even though I walk
through the valley of the shadow of death,

I will fear no evil,
for you are with me;
your rod and your staff,
they comfort me."

* Look - A Smile:
Your turn to be a Patti for someone else. How can you help?
What will they remember? Your turn also to find a Patti for
yourself. Let them offer advice, listen and care. Ask them to
remember.

* Let Go - A Surrender:
questions came quickly, quickly,
to me and from me,
but now i can remember
and now i can grasp that which hit me then,
which hit me so hard then,
then, when i could know nothing,
could not answer a what or a why
as they talked and i listened but learned so little,
in those moments of mystery
i knew only one thing to do:
to call on God, to cry out to God, to ask for His help;
and i did and He did.
and i live now,
and i look back and remember.
now i remember.

Chapter 9

* Listen - A Story:
Marilyn Williams now knows about cancer. She and her
family have learned so much since the doctor told her and Bob
the news. When that happens and a person has no insurance,
what can be done? What can be learned? The Williamses
learned so much.

Marilyn shares her lessons with us:

"Finding the lump was a shock. I poked and squeezed for

5 minutes before I was convinced it was really there. It is now only 4 1/2 months later, but I feel like I've lived a lifetime...and I wouldn't trade it if I could.

"The day the surgeon examined me, he knew it was malignant. My husband and I left the office and stepped into a new world. I have cancer. I didn't feel afraid, or mad, or worried, but I found myself wanting to cry. The tears never came out that day, and that was the first sign of how things were changing because, normally, I cry for everything.

"I believe God's promise that He only allows things to happen that will come to good. I believe God has a plan for each of us. For the first time in my life, I really had to live my words. We don't often get a chance to find out the depth of our faith and I found myself stripped of every crutch I had ever leaned on. My life, was in His hands, His hands alone. As we researched, got test results, did more research and asked questions that led to more questions...there was no denying it, my life was in His hands. This could go either way. Nothing in modern medicine could give me a guarantee, and just the treatment itself was pretty scary. What I discovered was that being in His hands is a wonderful place to be."

* Learn - A Strategy:
Take a friend on a trip. It is okay to go locally and with little expense. Just go. Make it a holiday, a birthday, a snow storm, a New York minute. Then write about how you noticed what you often ignore, and how your inner self can believe in snow again. Make plans about ways to fall in love with life.

* Lend - A Statement:
Luke 1:28-30 (NIV)
"The angel went to her and said, 'Greetings, you who are highly favored! The Lord is with you.'" Mary was greatly troubled at his words and wondered what kind of greeting this might be. But the angel said to her, 'Do not be afraid, Mary, you have found favor with God.'"

* Look – A Smile:
Find a stranger visiting your city. Look for a way to help. Give the lost directions. Encourage, inspire, invite. Let them feel welcome.

Also take time to help your friends deal with the stranger they might be internally. Study this list of words and pray for those struggling in such wars. Smile to encourage, inspire, and invite: antisocial, avoidant, impulsive, intrusive, compulsive, dependent, histrionic, narcissistic, paranoid, passive-aggressive, schizoid, schizotypal (*Coping With Mild Traumatic Brain Injury*, Diane Roberts Stoler, Ed.D., and Barbara Albers Hill, Avery, New York, 1998, pp. 208-209)

* Let Go – A Surrender:
I am staring at my family and a family of friends. I am in the room resting while they walk in a new world. This time, I'm not jealous. I am thankful. Here, alive, aware, awake, I am going to rest. I pray I pass the test.

Chapter 10

* Listen – A Story:
Joe Coffey also knows about pain. Listen to Joe's confession about his brother's death.

"I would never have guessed that I treated God as a household god until the death of my brother John. What you really believe comes out in how you live, especially in crisis. I watched helplessly as my theology crumbled. I was angry at this god I had served as a second-generation minister. What happened to our unspoken bargain? The agreement of a *quid pro quo* for services rendered? In time my understanding of God began to change. In my frustration and anger I reduced Him. I would allow for Him to be either powerful or loving, but I could not hold both of those in the same hand and offer them to Him in praise. Like a toddler I would reason that if God were both loving and powerful, I would not be in pain. I am grateful for the story of Jacob. I found myself invited into the wrestling ring with the One. It was an invitation I accepted, and for two years I threw myself at God with great fury. Finally I admitted I could not budge the 'unmoved mover' and surrendered. I surrendered to a God who refuses to be anything but who He is with thoughts and ways higher than high. It was a hard lesson but the best lesson I have learned. I am now thankful for hope and for impotence in the presence of Him who is able.

"John was 20, and I was 29. He didn't come home from work. He was living with me for the summer and working for college money. He had a motorcycle, and we had talked that weekend about how dangerous it could be. He had another 14-year-old from my youth group with him. Tim also died. I started calling the police and the highway patrol. They told me there had been a motorcycle accident but would not give me much information. They were trying to get someone to my house. I was alone because my wife, Karen, and our kids were on a trip. A highway patrolman pulled up, and I met him outside on my porch. He told me John had been killed and that Tim had died en route to the hospital. The hardest thing I have ever done in my life was to call my Dad and my brother. When I said that John was gone, my brother yelled like he had been hit. My Dad sighed, and I heard the life drain from him. When I saw him the next day, he looked like someone had cut the strings behind his face, and he was 10 years older. My Dad, my brother, and I went to the funeral home and stood with John before they worked on him. He still looked pretty normal. We cried about as hard as men can cry. It hurts to cry that much and that hard. It is like vomiting. That is what I remember."

* Learn - A Strategy:
"Meet with Jesus on a regular basis for conversation. Believe that he is truly present with you, assuming the theological truth that he inhabits the space all around you. Assume also that you are loved without measure." (*Falling For God*, Gary Moon, Shaw Books, 2004, p 125)

* Lend - A Statement:
Psalm 59:16 (NIV)
"But I will sing of your strength,
in the morning I will sing of your love;
for you are my fortress,
my refuge in times of trouble."

* Look - A Smile:
"Make a list of some things you know you should be doing
to foster conversation and communion with God, and do them
(obedience)." (*Falling For God*, p. 124)

* Let Go - A Surrender:
I remembered a song I wrote years ago, based on Psalm 46:
God is our refuge
Our help in time of trouble
Therefore we won't fear
Though the earth may give way
Though the mountains fall into the heart of the sea
Though the waters roar & foam
Though the mountains quake with surging
There is a river whose streams will make us glad

Chapter 11

* Listen - A Story:
Tim and Marie Kuck spent a Christmas in the hospital with
their son Nathaniel. It was his first Christmas. They watched
doctors and nurses and machines as the six-month-old child
struggled to survive. As they suffered, Tim and Marie also
heard their heavenly Father guide them to find ways of helping
others deal with seasonal battles of sickness and sadness. For
the next three years, the Kucks and many friends carried
Nathaniel back to the hospital on Christmas to sing, smile,
offer gifts and pray for patients and their families. Through
Nathaniel's multiple birth anomalies, surgeries, therapies,
feeding tubes, and special care, the Kucks learned so much

about how life really counts. Since four-year-old Nathaniel's passing to heaven on November 13, 2001, the Kucks have continued their holiday celebration of healing. Their ministry, Nathaniel's Hope, seeks to help families and friends realize those with disabilities really count.

http://www.nathanielshope.org/

* Learn - A Strategy:

Remember, you will never pass this way again. If you *could* live the last twelve months again, what would you change? Since you can't, what do you hope to do in the next twelve months to make this world a better place?

* Lend - A Statement:

Psalm 109:26 (NIV)

"Help me, O Lord my God;
save me in accordance with your love."

Isaiah 29:19 (*The Message*)

"The castoffs of society will be laughing and dancing in God, the down-and-outs shouting praise to The Holy of Israel."

* Look - A Smile:

Find people in need of care, of gifts, of smiles. Share your love and God's love with them.

* Let Go - A Surrender:

A year ends. A year begins. This will be a different year.
Maybe better, maybe worse. Maybe we will never know.
My concluding year came to me carrying a delightful cover. The beginning excited me, calmed me.
The change shifted me, but left me living.
I set goals for this new year. I take no guesses of what could occur.
This year, again, God remains God. I pray I know Him.

Chapter 12

* Listen - A Story:

Divorce. Talk about a loss, a change, a move. During my two decades of ministry and my four decades of life, I've heard the reasons. I've seen the results. This is not a time for debate or discussion. Just a confession of the pain that arrives in divorce.

A friend gave me permission to use her thoughts: "Chris, I listened to the world and myself. Now I live with so many regrets. I wanted to find something to make me feel better. Actually, I wanted someone to make me feel better. You told me not to, but I didn't listen. Please pray I allow God to forgive me and that I work to bring hope to myself and my torn apart family. Please pray."

* Learn - A Strategy:

Pray for families who have been torn apart. Pray for families who are legally still together but are actually far apart.

* Lend - A Statement:

2 Kings 12:2 (*The Message*)

"Taught and trained by Jehoiada the priest, Joash did what pleased God for as long as he lived."

* Look - A Smile:

List how you have been taught and trained even during the trials of life. Glance at your limitations. Then, face it. And let God grace it!

* Let Go - A Surrender:

Mysterious mistakes visited. Coming, going, sometimes showing ways of wrong or right. Trying to travel to the top—quickly, quickly—I grew tired. Worn out. Learning, though, learning how to move on through my life, my new life, with what is left in me, since what left me, subtracted.

God? Not gone, not distant. Good news? I learn from Him and lean on Him better. Do I have a choice? Sure. I could choose to wonder too long, too hard. I could live with Him at center, as Center, of my life, my focus. I want to, need to.

Chapter 13

* Listen - A Story:
List your painful life-changing experiences.

* Learn - A Strategy:
Make a list of reasons you are thankful God has spared your life. Think of ways God needs to do His editorial service to change you.

* Lend - A Statement:
2 Timothy 1:3 (NIV)
"I thank God, whom I serve, as my forefathers did, with a clear conscience, as night and day I constantly remember you in my prayers."

* Look - A Smile:
Write about how you have been made stronger. Consider ways of helping others become stronger.

* Let Go - A Surrender:
(lyrics by Chris Maxwell; music by Bill Tripp)

UNFAMILIAR TERRITORY
mysterious circumstances rise
to stare at me, visiting my demise
as involvement reaches a new place
i'm begging heaven for wonderful grace
hoping some help will come soon

caution jumps upward as fear arrives
and ventures violate such common lives
temptation, trials or tribulation

often surprise all my speculation
and challenge my private room

events can reflect only portions of facts
endurance can race through those attacks
enrichment can rescue our lives from our lacks
if we face unfamiliar territory
by turning to the glory
by turning to the glory of God

making plans that appear to exist
where my doubt will shout for me to resist
but i must sit still driving forward
as I'm unsure what I'm going toward
certain thoughts i must release

my mystery has some company
that has promised to give me victory
so i hold on to that assurance
and move forward with inner confidence
holding on to joy and peace

over time, emotions can rise
every line and every delay
must not depend on lies
to heal us and reveal us the way
to drift toward the skies
when our help knows today
we can face unfamiliar territory
by turning to the glory
by trusting, by releasing,
by receiving, by turning to the glory of God

Chapter 14

* Listen - A Story:
Read Christopher de Vinck's *The Power of the Powerless*. Ask yourself, "Whom do I really care about?"

* Learn - A Strategy:
What can you do to show that you care?

* Lend - A Statement:
Jeremiah 29:7 (NIV)
"Also, seek the peace and prosperity of the city to which I have carried you into exile. Pray to the Lord for it, because if it prospers, you too will prosper."

* Look - A Smile:
Today, move forward in a "ministry moment." Refuse to live packed with "missed opportunities." Remember: MM, not MO!

* Let Go - A Surrender:
Today, dear God,
Guide my hopes and selfish schemes
to peer beyond the in-betweens.
Then steer my love to life around me.
Each day, all day, help me to stay
in pace with You.
Can You help, heal?
Slow me down, make me real?
Dear God, today,
I pray You will.
(by Chris Maxwell, originally published in *Workday Prayers: On-the-job Meditations for Tending Your Soul*, by Timothy Jones, Loyola Press, 2000)

Chapter 15

* Listen - A Story:
Dr. Pineless once referred a patient to me. The man and his family struggled to adjust to a life-change experience. Dr. Pineless took care of the medical side. I joined with the family as we asked God to take care of the spiritual and relational side. The man wrote these words: "I had almost given up. Now I can keep going in life without being a quitter. I'm praying, reading

the Psalms and confessing my faults. And, as you said, I'm trying to enjoy the ride."

* Learn - A Strategy:

If you took yourself out to eat and interviewed you, what would you learn? What strengths and weaknesses should be discussed? How can you live with more hope?

* Lend - A Statement:

Romans 12:12 (NIV)

"Be joyful in hope, patient in affliction, faithful in prayer."

* Look - A Smile:

While eating out, make comments to give hope to others. Let their inner worlds smile.

* Let Go - A Surrender:

Am I listening,
Really listening,
To what matters?
To what really matters?
Am I learning,
Really learning,
About me?
About the real me?

Chapter 16

* Listen - A Story:

Dr. Attermann also has experienced such challenges personally. He told me how he felt when his daughter almost died at 3 1/2 years old. In a painful way, he could relate to Joseph's comments toward his frightened brothers: "It is not your fault. God has a grand plan."

A devout Jew, Dr. Attermann believes if we truly trust God the way Christians claim, then we depend on Him when nothing makes sense. He says, "Chris, I look at you now and consider you a soul mate. We have become friends as I watched you deal with disappointment."

After we stood together beside a friend as her husband died, we both felt more aware than ever that these bodies are not the end. God has a better plan and place for us. Until our times come, though, Dr. Attermann says, "We can adapt and face whatever tomorrow might bring. I've watched you do that."

* Learn - A Strategy:
Give yourself time to think through Dr. Pineless' words:
"The biggest problem is getting the patient to play by the rules and stick with it. Too many people just want instant gratification."

* Lend - A Statement:
Luke 8:47-48 (NIV)
"Then the woman, seeing that she could not go unnoticed, came trembling and fell at his feet. In the presence of all the people, she told why she had touched him and how she had been instantly healed. Then he said to her, 'Daughter, your faith has healed you. Go in peace.'"

* Look - A Smile:
View yourself as a gourmet chef. Smile at someone and serve. Just serve.

* Let Go - A Surrender:
How do the lights sound? How does the loudness shine? Who will know?
Now, in this place, in this time, in this.
Making sense out of sadness and taking growth from badness,
I will live on and on and on. Maybe. Maybe.
My God keeps me going, that One that keeps on knowing
so much more than each of us together. He knows.
Sometimes He shows
us what.
Often, He holds His wisdom. Hides His wisdom? Maybe. Maybe.

New days bring new ways. Am I a new man?
He is My Old God and My New God and My God.
See that? Hear that?
Us what?
Sometimes He shows.

Chapter 17

* Listen ‑ A Story:
Write a story about what you always hope to remember.
Write a story about what you long to forget.

* Learn ‑ A Strategy:
How is your memory these days? For those battling Mild
Traumatic Brain Injury, and for all people who struggle to
recall, realize the process of remembering is complex. It
involves three distinct phases: registration (or encoding),
storage and retrieval. (*Coping With Mild Traumatic Brain Injury*,
p. 150)
Write a story about you and your thoughts. Think about your
thinking. How can you stay better organized and keep a record
of what matters most? Work to make things work.

* Lend ‑ A Statement:
Acts 4:24, (NIV)
"When they heard this, they raised their voices together in
prayer to God. 'Sovereign Lord,' they said, 'you made the heaven
and the earth and the sea, and everything in them.'"

* Look ‑ A Smile:
Think about sensory memory (storage of information
lasting only seconds but leaving sights, smells or sounds), short‑
term memory (the part of memory that receives and recalls
information within one minute), and long‑term memory (the
information received and held beyond one minute.) Make a list
of what you remember that fits in each of those categories of
memory. Take time to smile about how God has helped you

in short-term and long-term events, as you remember. (*Coping With Mild Traumatic Brain Injury*, pp. 151-152)

* Let Go - A Surrender::

Hearing things. Responding incorrectly. Close to God. Acting wrong. My description of my disease differed from what I had heard. They told me about the brain, about brain problems, about medicine, about hard work to restructure thinking, about emotions. Emotions? Had they seen me cry? Yes, if they had seen me at all.

In the past, a laugher not a crier. In painful confusion, crying and misunderstanding gave so much. Often, unfortunate to family and close friends, I thought I grasped what I actually failed to grasp. Thinking I was so much better did not necessarily make me better. Time would, the experts told me. Some areas may never improve but I would learn how to face it, the experts told me. God loved me, that is what He told me. No specifics about the experts' opinions, no new ideas from what I heard. He reminded me in my heart, in my slow reading, in my close relationships, that He loved me. Was that not enough for me?

It had to be.

Some days I handled it fine. Other days, not so well.

So many days, so many sunny days, seemed cloudy, almost. Seeing life not so clearly reminded me of more than my weakness. It reminded me of God's strength.

Chapter 18

* Listen - A Story:

Jonathan Farrant remembers so much about his father, Peter, who served many years of ministry. God saved Peter's life many times as nationals tried to murder him. The miracles ended too soon, though. Read and learn from Jonathan's thoughts:

"In 1996 my family took a vacation/ministry trip to the Yucatan peninsula. We arrived in Mexico on December 20. We were excited to enjoy our time together. We fished all day in the ocean, catching fish after fish. This was the best trip of my life and soon would turn into my worst nightmare.

"On the third day we loaded up the vehicle to drive to a village where we would celebrate Christmas and my father's birthday. On the way to the village we passed many caves, and my brother pleaded to stop at every single one. Finally we found a cave that we would attempt to dive. There were many trees that surrounded what seemed to be a little pond, but in this pond was a huge cave that went for many miles. My father, brother, and I unloaded the two tanks and gear. My mom and sister waited in the car; our plan was to be back shortly. The three of us walked about a hundred yards to the pond and stood for a short while enjoying the beauty of God's creation. My brother and I began to suit up, excited to see what we could find. My father looked at me and said, 'Jonathan, let me go first, I will come up in ten minutes and then you can go.' I wasn't happy about waiting, but I figured ten minutes wasn't too bad. So I exchanged the gear with my father and he suited up. They got in this pond and went down to explore. I sat on a big rock waiting for them to come back up.

"After twenty minutes I thought something was wrong. I put my mask on and my snorkel and slowly tried to get in the cold water. Not having a wetsuit, it took me about ten minutes to get in. Over thirty minutes had passed by this time. Finally I swam over to the place where the cave began. As I got closer I could see my father. I said to myself, 'Good, he is finally coming out.' As I got closer I realized his BC wasn't in his mouth. I tried not to panic and I swam down about twenty feet. I grabbed him by the arm and dragged him up. When we got to the top I began to cry out, 'God, God, God!' I got myself together and I began to tell my father, 'You're going to be ok.' I pulled him to the shore. He was so heavy because he had inhaled so much water. I got him out and began to yell. I took off his tank, immediately performing CPR. My Mom and sister came and my Mom assisted with CPR. My sister cried as she watched us work with no success. He had gone to be with the Lord.

"I put on my mask and snorkel and cried out, 'Jethro!' I dove into the water but I could not see him anywhere. I swam as far as I could without an oxygen tank. There was no sign of my brother. I lay on my back in the water and cried. The best week of my life had turned out to be a complete tragedy.

"Hours later a rescue worker came, went into the cave, and took my brother's body out. The little hope of my brother still being alive was destroyed. I stared at my brother in disbelief and said, 'Get up now, let's go home.' But he had already gone to be with the Lord as well.

"I went on a long journey to receive restoration. I left everything that I'd known and moved where I wasn't known. From Florida, I moved to California, then Minnesota, then Illinois. No matter where I was in, the only place I could find peace was in the presence of my heavenly Father. The Lord used many things to heal my wounds. Through the years I discovered my purpose in life. Instead of staying in my corner, I decided I would make the most of my life. I discovered that no matter what I do or how much I cried, I couldn't bring them back. I stand with the hope that one day I will go to where my brother and father are, but before I get there I have a lot of work to do. Many people need to hear the gospel preached. Many lives need to be touched by the power of the Holy Spirit.

"The Lord has been faithful and has filled me with a great passion to minister. My wife and I have returned to the mission field where my father first started."

* Learn - A Strategy:
Write your own story about a weary person. Or about a time you have felt weary. End with an encouraging conclusion.

* Lend - A Statement:
Hebrews 4:16 (*The Message*)
"So let's walk right up to him and get what he is so ready to give. Take the mercy, accept the help."

Hebrews 4:16 (NIV)
"Let us then approach the throne of grace with confidence, so that we may receive mercy and find grace to help us in our time of need."

* Look - A Smile

Take time to smile someone's pain away. Pray, believing God's mercy and help can flow through you to them.

* Let Go - A Surrender:
Pain Drops (by Taylor Maxwell)

the pain drops to the floor
like the shower of one's tears
i don't feel that pain anymore
but, it plays along with my fears

come away with me tonight
fly up high and touch the sky
don't you ever go
beyond all comprehension
past all strife and tension
to believe?

the rain drops to the window pain
where the bibles laid for years
she reads the verse for the hundredth time
and she can't get His words off of her mind

come away with me tonight
fly up high and touch the sky
don't you ever go
beyond all comprehension
past all strife and tension
to believe?

to be alone right now
would only bring you down
stand up and look around
for He will help you out...

Chapter 19

* Listen - A Story:

I know a man who served in ministry many years. He has
encouraged me, challenged me, and dared me. He has also
told me not to make his mistake. He agreed to write about his
test—appropriate way to label a testimony--and titled it "A Man
Without a Church." Read it:

"When a pastor commits a moral sin, the magnitude of
that sin is so great that it has the capabilities of destroying the
calling itself, the ministry, the man, his marriage, his family, his
legacy, and the community where that moral failure took place.
In disgrace, humiliation, heartbreak, and nearly being tarred
and feathered, one man did that and was thrown out of town. I
was that man.

"I needed to lay aside ministry and regroup. In reality I was
a man without a ministry, a church, and an income. Not a nice
place to be. The transition from the religious/spiritual world
to the secular/non-religious world was not difficult. It was the
secular world that brought out innate skills that ultimately
would make me a better man – if only I could survive the
eight-year ordeal of getting my life back on track. It's called
Restoration.

"During this eight year wilderness journey there were six
individuals who were used by God to be part of His restoration
process. My life now of 69 years is a valid example of the
concept that even though we humans 'miss the mark': God uses
people, not the religious institution to restore us back into His
favor. This process is called God's grace."

* Learn - A Strategy:

Frederick Buechner, in *A Room Called Remember*,
(HarperCollins, 1992) wrote, "By grace we are on that way. By
grace there come unbidden moments when we feel in our bones
what it is like to be on that way."

I called Buechner two years after my illness. I told him
the new me loved his writing even more than the old me.
He wasn't sure about the newness or oldness, and he seemed

unsure about me loving his writing so much. He wanted to know why.

After mentioning his surprises, his use of words and his rhythm, I talked about his confessions. He reveals himself to his readers, refusing to hold his weariness into hiding. As I open his books, his words open me. I smile in motion as I flow through his honesty. I shake my head; I nod. His creative confessions make the short feel a little taller and the weak feel a little stronger. Reading his pages gave rest to this weary man.

* Lend - A Statement:
2 Corinthians 13:11 (NIV)
"Finally, brothers, good-by. Aim for perfection, listen to my appeal, be of one mind, live in peace. And the God of love and peace will be with you."

(Luke 22:32, KJV)
"But I have prayed for thee, that thy faith fail not: and when thou art converted, strengthen thy brethren."

* Look - A Smile:
Find a way to help a friend's dreams come true.

* Let Go - A Surrender:
Moments keep me guessing. My guesses keep me moving. Up, then down. I have previously lived with consistency and balance. Now I shift so suddenly.

Should I search for help within myself? Should I beg? Maybe pray regular prayers. Honest prayers unto a Father who already knows how I feel. Painful questions, honest frustration, shocking laughter, needed dreams. Unto Thee, O Lord. Unto. Thee. O. Lord. I lift up my sore self, my unsure self, my sad self; I lift up my soul. Singing and crying and talking, talking, talking. Waiting for an answer. Waiting for an end. Waiting for a beginning. Praying, not as a religious habit of words too far from me to relate to; praying as Psalms without the rhythm but with the honesty.

A visit of the past—that I needed. Rereading the many sermons I previously preached: messages of how Great God Almighty guides us through trouble, how He helps us through trouble, how He keeps us, keeps us, keeps us, how He wins the battle. I needed this reminder.

A Presence in the present and a promise for the future. The Spirit: here and now. The Word of God: for now and then. Emotions up and down, physical shifts too slow for my hopes, smiles from friends who care. Through it all—I remembered this song—I learn to trust in Jesus. Do I learn to trust in Jesus? Do I have any choice? I must and I shall. He will, He promised, help me remember.

Chapter 20

* Listen - A Story:

Tim and Peggy Edwards, pastors of Sharon Chapel in Glen Allan, Mississippi, also serve. Years ago, they traveled and sang for the Southern Gospel group *The Crusaders*. Peggy still writes songs and plays the keyboard. Her voice, though, can barely be heard. Surgeries and prayers have not healed her physical ailments. How can a talented singer still worship when her life is changed and her voice gone? Peggy whispers the answer: "We must trust God. We pray for healing, remembering God is our Shepherd. We are His sheep. He is the One in charge. Such thoughts bring healing to our spirits."

Peggy's correct. Handling life's disabilities with her words in mind can add spiritual health to pastors and churches. God prepares tables for us in the presence of our enemies. He leads us beside still waters and restores our souls.

* Learn - A Strategy:

Make a list of all the ways God has proved His great faithfulness. Give thanks for times you recognized His actions and responded correctly. Ask forgiveness for moments when you ignored His great faithfulness. Delete those files. Put together a plan to continue reminding yourself of God's faithfulness.

* Lend - A Statement:
Psalm 149:4, (NIV)
"For the Lord takes delight in his people;
he crowns the humble with salvation."

* Look - A Smile:
(*Charisma*, July 2004, used by permission)
When Healing Doesn't Come: **TRUST GOD**

Trust God. True faith doesn't force change to occur. It believes God knows best. It allows us to courageously endure. Even in a wheelchair. By facing reality, biblical faith brings victory no matter what the scoreboard says.

Receive help. When healing doesn't come, we can allow friends to fulfill their roles as teammates of Christ's body. We aren't called to do it all! We can maintain relationships and launch into new territory as a friend reminds us of a name, drives us to the doctor or feeds us a meal.

Understand how people might struggle with how we are "different." How can we love those trying to "like" us? Inner security and Divine Love. It is okay for them to resist change. Honestly confess that you also have to fight through it.

Stick to new rules. We expect children to follow guidelines. Two A's can help: Accept who you are; Adjust to the changes. Take the medicine. Make the appointments. If I have to use acronyms and rhymes, so what? If I have to use PowerPoint and PalmPilot, so what? Thank God for help. Even when we're bothered by limitations, submitting to what God has placed to save our lives helps us reach our potential for His glory.

Tell your story. That isn't being selfish. Many people need to learn what you know about change, recovery, hope. Why didn't you give up? Did you not have enough faith? Was it caused by sin? Announcing God's grace in your trial brings glory to Him and truth to His patients. Tell it!

Give time and talent to help those in need. To get more out of your battle, give more of yourself away. Use your strengths. Establish connections. Offer gifts, prayers and smiles. Hold a hand. Believe in a miracle.

Observe the many opportunities that now belong to the new you. Also use your weaknesses; Paul knew what he was writing about. God's strength shows off when we stand on the stage of life to facilitate an audience of hurting people.

Discharge hurt in healthy ways. Release inner infections of hate and anger. Don't deny them; send them away. Laugh and cry. I often have patients participate in what I call "Writing for the Health of It." Do that. Take David's Psalms and make them personal. Your journal isn't negative confession. It allows God to turn the mourning into dancing.

* Let Go - A Surrender:
Dear God. I give You thanks. I often ignore Your might. I let You leave my sight. For now, for this moment, I notice. Your faithfulness, Your ongoing and never stopping gush of glorious faithfulness, Your stormy and magnificent might of consistent faithfulness: I notice it. And I need it. So, today, I give praise to my Faithful Father, Friend and Healer.

Conclusion

STRENGTH FOR THE WEAK:
* Need help with your health? Contact Pam Smith:
Pam Smith, RD., L.D.N.
Nutritional Counseling Services
Dietitian, Nutritionist, Author and Speaker
Pam's *Living Well* Radio Program is heard on over 800 broadcast facilities worldwide.
407.896.4010
www.PamSmith.com

* The mission of Joni and Friends is to "communicate the Gospel and equip Christ-honoring churches worldwide to evangelize and disciple people affected by disability." They accomplish this by assisting persons with disability in their progress toward independence and fulfillment through a variety of programs that involve disability awareness, education, training, and printed resources, while offering

practical ways of serving disabled persons and their families.

Joni and Friends
PO Box 3333
Agoura Hills, CA 91376
818-707-5664
www.joniandfriends.org
Email: rcrdept@joniandfriends.org

* Rest Ministries, Inc. is a non-profit Christian organization that exists to serve people who live with chronic illness or pain, and their families, by providing spiritual, emotional, relational, and practical support through a variety of resources, including *HopeKeepers Magazine*®, HopeKeepers groups, and small group materials. We also seek to bring an awareness and a change in action throughout churches in the U.S., in regard to how people who live with chronic illness or pain are served, and teach churches effective ministry tools in ministering to this population. Sponsor National Invisible Chronic Illness Awareness Week annually in September.

Rest Ministries
http://www.restministries.org
PO Box 502928, San Diego, CA 92150
Toll-free 888-751-7378
FAX 800-933-1078

* What about help with for those with cancer and amputations? The mission of Dave Dravecky's Outreach of Hope is to serve suffering people, especially those with cancer and amputation, by offering resources for encouragement, comfort and hope through a personal relationship with Jesus Christ.

Dave Dravecky's Outreach of Hope provides prayer support, non-medical referral services and resources for churches, healthcare professionals and individuals who work with those who suffer. For more information contact:

13840 Gleneagle Drive
Colorado Springs, CO 80921
Phone: 719-481-3528 Fax: 719-481-4689
E-mail: info@OutreachOfHope.org
Internet: www.OutreachOfHope.org

* Suggested reading:
Coping with Mild Traumatic Brain Injury, Dianne Roberts Stoler, Ed.D, and Barbara Albers Hill, Avery, 1998.

Endnotes

[1] Floyd Skloot, *The Night-Side: The Chronic Fatigue Syndrome and the Illness Experience,* Story Line Press, 1996, p. xiv

[2] R. T. Kendall, *The Thorn in the Flesh,* Charisma House, 2004, p. 87.

[3] Annie Dillard, *An American Childhood*, Harper & Row, 1987.

[4] Annie Dillard, *Pilgrim at Tinker Creek*, HarperCollins, 1974.

[5] Annie Dillard, *Pilgrim at Tinker Creek.*

[6] Cecil Murphey, *Committed But Flawed*, Living Ink Books, 2004, p. 41.

[7] Joni Eareckson Tada, *Choices...Changes*, Zondervan, 1986, p. 89

[8] Floyd Skloot, *The Night-Side: The Chronic Fatigue Syndrome and the Illness Experience,* Story Line Press, 1996, p. xii.

[9] V.S. Ramachandran and Sandra Blakeslee, *Phantoms in the Brain: Probing the Mysteries of the Human Mind,* William Morrow, 1998.

[10] *Coping With Mild Traumatic Brain Injury*, Diane Roberts Stoler, Ed.D., and Barbara Albers Hill, Avery, New York, 1998, p. 216.

[11] *Coping With Mild Traumatic Brain Injury*, Diane Roberts Stoler, Ed.D., and Barbara Albers Hill, Avery, New York, 1998, p. 218.

[12] *Coping With Mild Traumatic Brain Injury*, Diane Roberts Stoler, Ed.D., and Barbara Albers Hill, Avery, New York, 1998, p. 221.

[13] Mark Rutland, *Hanging By a Thread*, Creation House, 1991, p. 24.

[14] Portions of this chapter appeared in *Ministries Today*; other portions appeared in *Leadership Journal*.

[15] Insufficient Memory at This Time™ is a ComputerGear trademark. ComputerGear, 4028 148th Ave NE Redmond WA 98052 425-883-9052, http://www.computergear.com.

[16] Anne Lamott, *Bird by Bird*, Anchor Books, New York, 1994, pp. 106-107.

[17] Calvin Miller, *Into the Depths of God*, Bethany House, 2000, p. 129.

[18] *Coping With Mild Traumatic Brain Injury*, Diane Roberts Stoler, Ed.D., and Barbara Albers Hill, Avery, New York, 1998, p. 7.

[19] *Coping With Mild Traumatic Brain Injury*, Diane Roberts Stoler, Ed.D., and Barbara Albers Hill, Avery, New York, 1998, pp. 149-150.

[20] *Eugene H. Peterson,* Leap Over a Wall: Earthy Spirituality for Everyday Christians, HarperSanFrancisco, 1998.

[21] Portions of this chapter appeared in *IssacharFile* and *Revelation*.

[22] Leonard Sweet, *Summoned to Lead*, Zondervan, 2004, p. 96.

[23] Calvin Miller, *The Singer*, InterVarsity Press, Downers Grove, Illinois, 1975, p. 47.

[24] Dave Dravecky w/ Tim Stafford, *Comeback,* Zondervan, 1990, p 122.